Anti-Cancer Diet

The Top 99 Delicious Recipes To Fight Cancer And Restore Your Health

"Great Books Change Life"

Table of Contents

Introduction

I would like to take this opportunity to thank you for purchasing this book, *"Anti-Cancer Diet: The Top 50 delicious recipes to fight cancer and live a healthy life,"* and hope you find it informative and helpful in your endeavor to learn more about how you can keep cancer at bay by eating right.

Food plays a major role in maintaining a healthy lifestyle. Time and again, it has been proven that the food we consume has a direct impact on our total body health condition. Right food, regular exercise and plenty of water will help you feel younger and healthier. Unfortunately, the modern-day diet has taken a toll on the body by making diseases like cancer, diabetes, etc. very common. Do you want to keep yourself free from these deadly diseases? Especially cancer? It is definitely possible by including plant-based diets, exercise and a positive attitude to your regular lifestyle.

Cancer affects millions of people every year globally and there are many causes for the same, but the main reason which is closely linked to this disease is – lack of physical activity and proper nutritional diet. "Too much" and "Too little" dietary habits tend to increase our cancer risk. Too much red meat, alcohol, smoking, fried food, dairy, sugars, refined carbohydrates and too little physical activity, whole grains, phytochemical rich plant foods, fiber based fruits are the reasons for cancer.

Following the anti-cancer diet on a regular basis is the best way to reduce your risk of cancer. It is not possible to change your diet overnight but it is definitely possible when you take it slowly and gradually work it up. Most of the plant-based foods are immune based foods and have a high nutritional quotient. In this book, we will discuss the simple and possible ways to have an anti-cancer diet in our daily lifestyle and try to live a cancer-free life.

The chapters will discuss about the possible combination of vegetables, fruit and cereals we can have on a regular basis. We will also be helping you with few simple recipes to make your daily meal interesting.

I hope this simple cookbook will help you with an easy way to modify your regular diet and have a stress-free healthy lifestyle. Thanks once again for purchasing this book. I hope this book serves as an informative and interesting read for you!

Chapter 1: Role of Food in Tackling Cancer

What is cancer? To make it simple – "an abnormal growth." How does it happen? An uncontrolled cell division leads to tumor or abnormal cell growth i.e., when the tumor cells grow and divide beyond any control, they invade the tissues around the tumor and eventually spread to other body parts including your lymphatic systems and blood leading to painful or painless growth in the body. How do you avoid or control this? Consuming plenty of anti-cancer foods with antioxidants and natural anti-inflammatory phytonutrients can help reduce the risk of cancer.

Before discussing the anti-cancer diet chart, you need to understand and be very clear on your current food consumption and the dangerous food items that need to be completely avoided.

Food to avoid

Foods contributing to cancer usually include pesticides, preservatives, chemicals, animal products, artificial sweeteners, additives and dairy. It is a no brainer that we should be keeping away from these elements. However, we knowingly or unknowingly end up eating food laced with these products. Our fast food habits are the biggest cause of the consumption of these cancer-causing foods, which should be avoided at cost.

To be more specific, the following cancer causing foods must definitely be avoided from your regular diet

Processed meat
The meat you consume is full of hormones and preservatives to prolong shelf life and to improve taste. Processed meat should be left back on the shelf at the supermarket.

Red meat
It has already been proven that consumption of red meat is directly linked to a "high risk of cancer." Of course, I would not ask to completely avoid red meat but you can definitely lower the amount you consume.

Soda
Why drink it when you know it is loaded with sugar, artificial ingredients and calories that have no nutrition? Sadly, a lot of us are addicted to these sugary colas, which doesn't help your body in any way. You need to cut out sodas completely as soon as possible.

Fried / overly cooked food
Acrylamide, which is cancerous, is formed when the food is heated to a high temperature. Most food loses its nutrition when fried at a high temperature. Instead, try roasting your food.

Added sugar / artificial sweeteners
High consumption of added sugar can increase the risk of esophageal cancer, small intestine cancer, colon cancer and breast cancer.

Microwave popcorn

Chemicals in this popcorn can cause testicular, pancreatic and liver cancer. You can instead use popcorn kernels that are not dabbed in butter or any flavor and instead pop them in a wide bottomed pan with a bit of olive oil, salt and turmeric.

Processed food

Processed food usually contains dietary emulsifiers, which increase tumor formation, low-grade inflammation and colon carcinogenesis.

Cancer fighting food

Most of the plant-based food has phytonutrients that naturally prevent the human body from contracting various diseases.

Consciously including the below mentioned cancer fighting foods will reduce the risk of cancer in your life:

- Garlic
- Berries
- Tomatoes (Cooked)
- Cruciferous vegetables (Broccoli, Cabbage, Cauliflower)
- Green tea
- Whole grains
- Turmeric
- Leafy green vegetables (Spinach, Lettuce, Mustard greens, Collard greens, etc.)
- Grapes
- Beans
- Carrots
- Salads and green juices
- Unrefined oils

Cancer prevention tips

Your diet and its quality of life are linked to your health and its ability to prevent cancer. Apart from having a nutritional diet, there are few other things that are important to prevent cancer. Regular exercise, avoiding frequent medication, putting an end to smoking, reducing alcohol consumption, proper sleep and controlling your stress are the other things which needs to be on your "to-do" list.

Do check out the following and try implementing them:

- Have a fruit-rich diet to avoid lung and stomach cancer
- Add vegetables rich in carotenoids (carrots, sprouts, ripe tomatoes) to prevent larynx cancer, pharynx cancer, lung cancer and mouth cancer.
- Eat non-starchy vegetables (spinach, beans, broccoli) to avoid esophageal and stomach cancer
- Vitamin C rich foods (bell peppers, peas, leafy greens, berries, oranges,) can help avoid esophageal cancer
- Consume foods rich in lycopene (tomatoes, guava, watermelon,) to avoid prostate cancer

Focus on a healthy nutritious lifestyle to lead a stress free life. To ensure you follow your anti-cancer diet religiously, talk to your body, understand its needs, help your body with the cleansing and detoxifying process, drink loads of water, give enough Vitamin D to your body, eat organic and unprocessed food.

Chapter 2:
Anti-Cancer Smoothie Recipes

Anti-Cancer Breakfast Smoothie

Broccoli and strawberries are excellent sources of anti-oxidants and vitamin C. Strawberries are having quercetin that destructs cancer cells.

Preparation time: 5 minutes

Number of servings: 1-2

Ingredients:

- 2 tablespoons hemp seeds
- 1 small ripe banana, sliced
- ¼ cup frozen or fresh pomegranate arils
- 2 cups salad greens or kale or spinach or collard greens
- 1 tablespoon cocoa powder
- ½ tablespoon ground chia seeds
- Juice of ½ lime
- 1 ½ cups filtered water
- ½ cup frozen strawberries
- ½ inch fresh ginger, sliced
- A handful fresh mint leaves
- 1 tablespoon flax meal
- ¼ cup frozen raw broccoli florets

Directions:

- If you are using kale or spinach or collard greens, then steam it for 5-6 minutes.
- Cool completely.
- Add hemp seeds and water into a blender and blend for 12-15 seconds.
- Add strawberries, banana and pomegranate and blend for another 12-15 seconds.
- Add cocoa, mint leaves, flax meal, broccoli, chia seeds, lime juice ginger and the greens that you are using. Blend for 30-40 seconds or until smooth. Add more water if you like a smoothie of thinner consistency.
- Pour into tall glass and serve with crushed ice right away.

Super Healthy Smoothie

Goji berries help in increasing the body's immunity and energy. They are high in carotenoids. All bright colored fruit and vegetables are high in carotenoids and are essential for building the immunity of the body.

Preparation time: 10 minutes

Number of servings: 1-2

Ingredients:

- 2 -3 tablespoons goji berries
- 20 raspberries
- 1 small avocado, peeled, pitted chopped
- ½ small beetroot, peeled, chopped
- 20 seedless red grapes
- 4 small broccoli florets
- 1 ½ cups coconut water or water
- 1 teaspoon olive oil

Directions:

- Add goji berries, raspberries, avocado, beetroot, grapes, broccoli, olive oil and coconut water into a blender and blend for 30-40 seconds or until smooth. Add more coconut water if you like your smoothie to be thinner in consistency.
- Pour into a tall glass and serve with crushed ice.

Green Smoothie

Spinach, romaine lettuce and kale are excellent sources of beta-carotene and vitamin C. Ginger is known to prevent cancer and inhibit tumor cell growth.

Preparation time: 10 minutes

Number of servings: 2

Ingredients:

- 2 medium bananas, sliced, frozen
- 2 cups spinach, torn
- 2 cups kale leaves, discard hard ribs and stem
- 2 cups celery, chopped
- 2 cups romaine lettuce, torn
- A handful mint leaves
- A handful fresh parsley
- 2 inch piece fresh ginger, sliced
- 2 medium cucumbers, chopped
- 2 small pear or Granny Smith apple, cored, chopped, peel if desired
- 1 teaspoon ground cinnamon
- 4 tablespoons lemon juice
- 1 tablespoon chia seeds
- A pinch cayenne pepper
- 2 cups coconut water or water
- Natural sweetener like stevia or honey (optional), to

Directions:

- Add banana, spinach, kale, celery, lettuce, mint parsley, ginger, cucumber, pear or apple, cinnamon, lemon juice, chia seeds, cayenne pepper, coconut water and sweetener if using into a blender and blend until smooth.

- Add more coconut water if you desire a smoothie of thinner consistency.
- Pour into a tall glass and serve with crushed ice.

Orange Wheatgrass Smoothie

Wheat grass is known to prevent cancer. It is loaded with vitamins, minerals is an anti-oxidant.

Preparation time: 5 minutes

Number of servings: 2

Ingredients:

- ½ cup water or coconut water
- ½ cup fresh wheatgrass or ½ teaspoon wheatgrass powder
- 1 banana, peeled, sliced, frozen
- 1 cup almond milk or soy milk
- 2 oranges or 4 tangerines, peeled (the thin membrane from the segments as well), deseeded
- 1 cup ice

Directions:

- Add the ingredients into a blender in the order mentioned – coconut water, almond milk, wheat grass, tangerine, banana and ice.
- Blend for 30-40 seconds or until smooth. Add more coconut water if you want a smoothie of thinner consistency.
- Pour into tall glasses and serve.

Red Smoothie

Turmeric contains curcumin, which is anti-cancerous. It is also known to reduce the size of tumors.

Preparation time: 5 minutes

Number of servings: 2

Ingredients:

- 1 banana, sliced, frozen
- 4 stalks kale, discard hard stems and ribs, torn
- 1 inch fresh ginger, peeled, sliced
- ½ teaspoon turmeric powder
- 1 teaspoon organic coconut oil
- 2 teaspoons black nigella seeds
- ¼ cup raspberries
- 4 strawberries, chopped
- 2 carrots, chopped
- 2 cups red cabbage, shredded
- A pinch black pepper
- 2 teaspoons chia seeds
- 2 cups almond milk
- Ice cubes, as required

Directions:

- Add banana, kale, ginger, turmeric powder, coconut oil, nigella seeds, raspberries, strawberries, carrots, red cabbage, pepper, chia seeds, almond milk and ice cubes into a blender.

- Blend for 30-40 seconds or until smooth. Add more almond milk if you like a smoothie of thinner consistency.
- Pour into tall glasses and serve.

Green Super Foods Smoothie

Probiotic foods stop the growth of tumors and help in cell growth. Chia seeds and wheatgrass powder are anti-cancerous.

Preparation time: 10 minutes

Number of servings: 3-4

Ingredients:

- 2 green tea bags
- 1 cup unfiltered apple juice
- 2 medium bananas, sliced
- 4 tablespoons lemon juice
- 4 teaspoons wheatgrass powder
- 4 cups frozen pineapple chunks, unsweetened
- 2 cups hot water
- 1 teaspoon probiotic powder
- 6 tablespoons sprouted chia seed powder
- 2 cups firmly packed baby spinach
- 2 tablespoons hemp seed protein powder
- A pinch Celtic sea salt

Directions:

- Drop the tea bags in hot water for a minute. Discard the tea bags and cool completely.
- Pour the brewed tea into a blender. Add apple juice, banana, lemon juice, wheatgrass powder, pineapple,

probiotic powder, chia seed powder, spinach, hemp seed powder and salt into a blender.

- Blend for 30-40 seconds or until smooth. Add more water if you like a smoothie of thinner consistency.
- Pour into tall glasses and serve with crushed ice.

Chapter 3:
Anti-Cancer Juice Recipes

Tomato Juice

Tomatoes help in preventing the DNA in the cells from getting damaged. Tomatoes are high in lycopene. Garlic and ginger help in preventing cancer.

Preparation time: 10 minutes

Number of servings: 2

Ingredients:

- 8 tomatoes, chopped into chunks
- 1 bell pepper, deseeded, chopped into chunks
- 4 stalks celery, chopped into pieces
- 1 small bunch parsley
- 1 small bunch cilantro
- 2 inch piece fresh ginger, peeled, sliced
- 4 tablespoons lemon juice
- 2 cloves garlic, peeled

Directions:

- Juice together tomatoes, bell pepper, celery, parsley, and cilantro, and ginger, garlic and lemon juice in a juicer.
- Alternately, you can add all the ingredients into a blender and blend until smooth.

- Strain if desired.
- Pour into tall glasses and serve with crushed ice.

Vibrant Green Ginger Tonic

This green juice is full of antioxidants, vitamins and minerals. Kale celery and parsley contain lots of it.

Preparation time: 10 minutes

Number of servings: 2

Ingredients:

- Juice of 2 lemons
- 3 inch piece of ginger, peeled, chopped
- A pinch of salt
- 2 green apples, cored, sliced
- 10 stalks of celery, chopped
- 10 kale leaves, discard hard stems and ribs, torn
- 2 handfuls parsley
- Lemon zest to garnish

Directions:

- Juice together ginger, apple, celery, kale and parsley in a juicer
- Alternately, you can add the ingredients into a blender and blend until smooth.
- Strain if desired.
- Pour into tall glasses. Add lemon juice and stir.
- Garnish with lemon zest.
- Sprinkle with a pinch of salt and cayenne pepper if you like it spicy. Serve with ice cubes.

Sunrise Juice

Bright colored fruit and vegetables are high in vitamin C and beta-carotene.

Preparation time: 10 minutes

Number of servings: 2

Ingredients:

- 2 medium sized pink grapefruit, peeled, deseeded
- 2 apples, cored, sliced
- 8 medium carrots, chopped
- 2 inch piece ginger, sliced
- Juice of a lemon

Directions:

- Juice together grapefruit, apples, carrots and ginger into a juicer. Add lemon juice and stir.
- Alternately, you can add the ingredients into a blender and blend until smooth.
- Strain if desired.
- Pour into tall glasses. Add lemon juice and stir.
- Serve with ice.

Tornado Juice

Citrus fruit is high in vitamin C. Tomatoes have lycopene.

Preparation time: 12-15 minutes

Number of servings: 2

Ingredients:

- 2 oranges, peeled, separated into segments
- ½ lemon, peeled, deseeded
- 2 medium carrots, chopped
- 4 stalks celery, chopped
- 2 cucumbers, chopped
- 2 apples, cored, chopped
- 2 inches fresh ginger, sliced
- 1 cup spinach
- 2 cups cherry tomatoes

Directions:

- Juice together oranges, lemon, carrots, celery, cucumbers, apples, ginger, spinach and cherry tomatoes in a juicer.
- Alternately, you can add the ingredients into a blender and blend until smooth.
- Strain if desired.
- Pour into tall glasses.
- You can either have it plain or even hot. It tastes good with ice too.

Papaya Pineapple Blast

Bright colored fruit is oozing with phytochemicals. Cashew nuts are full of healthy fatty acids. This juice is full of vitamin C that keeps your immunity strong.

Preparation time: 15 minutes

Number of servings: 2

Ingredients:

- 1 cup pomegranate arils
- 1 cup ripe papaya chunks
- 1 cup pineapple chunks
- 6 strawberries, chopped
- 2 cups mixed greens
- 10 cashew nuts
- 1 teaspoon coconut oil
- 2 cups coconut water

Directions:

- Juice together pomegranate arils, papaya, pineapple, strawberries, mixed greens, cashew nuts, coconut oil and coconut water in a juicer.
- Alternately, you can add the ingredients into a blender and blend until smooth.
- Strain if desired.
- Pour into tall glasses.
- Serve with crushed ice.

Purple Power Juice

Red cabbage is a cruciferous vegetable that is anti-cancerous. Purple grapes are high in resveratrol, which is anti-cancerous.

Preparation time: 10 minutes

Number of servings: 2

Ingredients:

- 2 cucumbers, chopped
- 4 stalks celery, chopped
- 2 Granny Smith apples, cored, chopped
- 2 cups purple grapes
- 2 inch piece fresh ginger, chopped
- 2 carrots, chopped
- 2 beets, sliced
- Greens of 2 beets, chopped
- 1 small red cabbage, cut into wedges

Directions:

- Add cucumber, celery, apples, grapes, ginger, carrots, beets, beet greens and cabbage into a blender and blend until smooth.
- Strain if desired.
- Alternately, juice together in a juicer.
- Pour into tall glasses and serve with ice.

Chapter 4: Anti-Cancer Breakfast Recipes

Quinoa Porridge

Quinoa is rich in protein and all the essential amino acids. Sugar is well utilized in the body with cinnamon. The sugar quickly goes from the blood into the cells to use as energy.

Preparation time: 10 minutes

Number of servings: 6

Ingredients:

- 2 cups quinoa, rinsed
- 4 cups water
- 6 teaspoons ground cinnamon
- 1 cup dried cranberries or currants
- 1 cup hemp hearts
- Maple syrup or honey to taste
- 2 cups coconut milk
- 4 cups water
- 3 teaspoons ground ginger
- 4 apples, cored, chopped
- 1 cup walnuts, chopped

Directions:

- Add quinoa, water, ginger, cinnamon, coconut milk, cranberries and apples into a heavy bottomed pan.

- Place the pan over medium heat. Bring to the boil.
- Lower heat and cover with a lid. Simmer until quinoa is cooked and all the water is dry.
- Divide into bowls. Sprinkle walnuts and hemp hearts. Top with honey or maple syrup and serve.

Pumpkin-Papaya Acai Bowl

Pumpkin is low in calories. It is high in potassium, fiber, phytoestrogens and beta-carotene and protects the body against free radicles, which is the major cause for cancer.

Preparation time: 10 minutes

Number of servings: 6

Ingredients:

For the acai bowl:

- 1 cup papaya, chopped into chunks
- 1 cup canned pumpkin
- 2 medium bananas, sliced
- 2 frozen acai smoothie pack, unsweetened
- 1 tablespoon ground cinnamon
- 1 tablespoon pumpkin pie spice
- 2 tablespoons maca powder
- 2 cups almond milk

To serve:

- 1 cup goji berries
- ½ cup cashews, chopped, toasted
- A few slices papaya
- A few slices banana
- ½ cup pomegranate seeds
- ½ cup granola

Directions:

- Add papaya, pumpkin, banana, acai smoothie pack, cinnamon, pumpkin pie spice, maca powder and almond milk into the blender and blend until smooth. Pour into 6 serving bowls. Chill if desired.
- Add papaya and banana slices and pomegranate seeds and stir.
- Sprinkle goji berries, cashews and granola on top and serve right away.

Veggie Egg Muffins

Turmeric has curcumin, which is an anti-oxidant and promotes apoptosis (cancer cells are killed). Spinach and bright colored bell peppers are great anti-cancer foods.

Preparation time: 15 minutes

Number of servings: 6

Ingredients:

- 6 eggs
- 1 large tomato, chopped
- ½ teaspoon turmeric powder
- 1 large onion, chopped
- 2 cloves garlic, minced
- 1 orange or red bell pepper, chopped
- ½ cup spinach, chopped
- Salt and Pepper as per taste
- A handful fresh basil, chopped

Directions:

- Grease 6 muffin cups. Place disposable liners in them.
- Add eggs and coconut milk in a medium bowl and whisk the contents well. Add turmeric, salt and pepper and whisk well.
- Add onion, bell pepper, spinach and tomatoes and stir.
- Spoon into the muffin cups. Fill up to ¾.

- Bake in a preheated oven at 350° F for 15 minutes or until set. A toothpick when inserted in the center should come out clean.
- Let it remain in the oven for 10 minutes.
- Remove from the oven and cool for a while. Run a knife around the edges to loosen the muffins. Invert on to a plate.
- Serve warm.

Cauliflower Pancakes

Eggs contain choline and it reduces the risk of cancer especially breast cancer. Cauliflower is a cruciferous vegetable that is highly beneficial in fighting cancer.

Preparation time: 10 minutes

Number of servings: 3

Ingredients:

- 1 large head cauliflower, broken into florets
- 3 tablespoons flat leaf parsley, chopped
- 3 eggs
- ¾ cup leeks, cleaned, chopped
- ¾ cup almond flour
- 2 cups smoked gouda cheese, shredded (optional)
- Salt to taste
- Pepper powder to taste
- 4-5 tablespoons coconut oil
- Eggs for serving

Directions:

- Place cauliflower florets in the food processor bowl and pulse until you get rice like texture. Alternately you can grate it. Transfer into a bowl.
- Place a skillet over low heat and add ½ tablespoon oil. When the oil is heated, add leeks and sauté until translucent.

- Add garlic and sauté for a few seconds until fragrant. Remove from heat and transfer into the bowl of cauliflower. Mix well.
- Add parsley, salt, pepper, almond flour, 3 eggs and Gouda cheese if using. Mix until well combined.
- Place a nonstick pan over low heat and add ½ teaspoon oil. When oil is heated, add about a heaping tablespoonful of cauliflower mixture on the pan and spread a little using the back of a spoon.
- Cook until the underside is golden brown. Flip sides and cook the other side too.
- Remove on to a serving platter.
- Repeat step 5 and 6 to make the remaining pancakes
- Cook eggs sunny side up. Serve pancakes with eggs.

Power up Breakfast Burrito

Low fat cheese helps in reducing the risk of colon cancer. Spinach or kale is anti-cancerous. Berries are high in anti-oxidants.

Preparation time: 10 minutes

Number of servings: 4

Ingredients:

- 4 teaspoons olive oil
- 2 cups fresh spinach or kale, shredded
- 3-4 tablespoons skim milk
- 4 whole wheat tortillas
- 1 medium red onion, chopped (optional)
- 4 eggs
- 4 ounces low fat mozzarella cheese, shredded
- Berries to serve
- Salt to taste
- Pepper to taste

Directions:

- Place a skillet over low heat and add oil. When the oil is heated, add onion and sauté until translucent.
- Add spinach and sauté until it turns bright green in color.
- Meanwhile, add eggs and milk into a bowl. Whisk well.

- Pour into the skillet along with mozzarella. Stir frequently until the eggs are scrambled and cooked. Season with salt and pepper
- Warm the tortillas following the instructions on the package.
- Spread the tortillas on a serving platter. Divide the mixture among the 4 tortillas. Do not place filling on the sides.
- Fold the bottom of the tortilla. Fold the sides together. Roll the tortillas.
- Wrap in paper towels.
- Serve with berries of your choice.

Green Tea-Scented Quinoa with Corn

Green tea has catechins, which are antioxidants that are highly anti-cancerous, and destroys the cancer cells. Quinoa, broccoli sprouts and carrots are high in anti-oxidants.

Preparation time: 14 minutes

Number of servings: 2

Ingredients:

- ½ cup quinoa, rinsed
- Salt to taste
- 2 tablespoons fresh or frozen corn kernels
- 1 clove garlic, minced
- 1 teaspoon lemon juice
- 2 sprigs parsley, chopped
- 1 teaspoon flaxseed oil
- Fistful broccoli sprouts
- 1 cup lightly brewed green tea
- 14 cup scallion, finely chopped
- ¼ cup carrot, finely chopped

Directions:

- Add quinoa and green tea into a saucepan. Place the saucepan over medium heat. Bring to the boil.
- Add corn, scallion, salt, garlic and carrot and stir.
- Lower heat and cover with a lid. Simmer until dry.

- Add parsley, lemon juice and flaxseed oil and loosen with a fork.
- Garnish with broccoli sprouts and serve.

Chapter 5:
Anti-cancer Snack Recipes

Sweet Potato Fries

Sweet potatoes have loads of beta-carotene, fiber, vitamin C etc. They reduce the risk of lung cancer, colon cancer, breast cancer and stomach cancer.

Preparation time: 10 minutes

Number of servings: 4

Ingredients:

- 4 medium sweet potatoes, scrubbed or peeled, sliced into julienne strips
- 1 teaspoon chili powder
- 1 teaspoon pepper powder
- 1 teaspoon ground cumin
- ½ teaspoon cayenne pepper
- Sea salt to taste
- 2 tablespoons extra virgin olive oil

Directions:

- Add sweet potatoes, chili powder, cumin, pepper, and cayenne pepper, salt into a bowl and toss well.
- Drizzle oil on top and toss well.
- Transfer on to a greased baking sheet and spread it in a single layer.

- Bake in a preheated oven 425° F for about 30 minutes or until the top is light brown in color. It should be tender inside and crisp outside. Turn the sweet potatoes half way through baking.
- Serve hot with a dip of your choice.

Cheese Balls

Goat's cheese and chia seeds are nutrient dense. Chia seeds and almonds are high in fiber and omega– 3 fatty acids.

Preparation time: 15 minutes

Number of servings: 6 (3 balls each)

Ingredients:

- 4 ounces plain almond milk cream cheese
- 4 ounces goat's cheese
- ¼ teaspoon garlic, minced
- A handful fresh cilantro, finely chopped
- ¼ cup roasted, salted almonds, chopped
- 4 teaspoons chia seeds
- Pepper powder to taste
- Salt to taste

Directions:

- Add goat's cheese and cream cheese into a bowl.
- Beat with an electric mixer on medium speed until smooth.
- Add cilantro, salt, pepper and garlic and mix. Place the bowl in the freezer for 15 minutes.
- Add nuts into the food processor bowl and pulse until fine. Transfer into a bowl. Add chia seeds and mix.
- Divide the mixture into 18 equal portions and shape into balls.
- Dredge the balls in the nut mixture. Place in an airtight container and refrigerate until use.
- Serve with a dip of your choice.

Spinach Rolls with Ricotta & Pistachios

Spinach is high in vitamin C and A. These are anti-bacterial and anti-viral and have the capability to prevent formation of tumors.

Preparation time: 10 minutes

Number of servings: 8

Ingredients:

- 4 tablespoons extra virgin olive oil, divided
- 18 ounces fresh spinach, rinsed, discard tough stems, finely chopped
- 14 ounces part skim ricotta
- ½ cup low fat parmesan cheese, grated, divided
- 1 teaspoon ground nutmeg
- 8 whole wheat lasagna sheets, cook according to the instructions on the package
- 2 cups pistachio nuts, finely chopped
- Salt to taste

Directions:

- Place a skillet over low heat and add half the oil. When the oil is heated, add spinach and salt and sauté until the spinach wilts.
- Remove from heat and cool completely. Transfer into a bowl.
- Add ricotta, half the Parmesan, nutmeg, and pistachio nuts and salt and set aside.

- Dry the cooked lasagna sheets with paper towels. Place a lasagna sheet on your countertop.
- Spread the cheese mixture over it. Roll and set aside.
- Repeat with the remaining mixture and lasagna sheets.
- Cut into slices of about 1-2 inches. Drizzle the remaining oil over it and sprinkle the remaining cheese on top and serve.
- If you like the cheese melted, microwave on high for a few seconds until the cheese melts and serve.

Vegan Spinach Balls

Spinach is an antioxidant and detoxifies your body.

Preparation time: 5 minutes

Number of servings: 10

Ingredients:

- 1 ½ cups fresh spinach
- ½ cup almonds
- ¼ cup cashews
- 1 ½ tablespoons olive oil
- ½ tablespoon chia seeds or flax seeds mixed with 1 ½ tablespoons water (egg replacer)
- ¼ cup oats
- ¼ teaspoon salt
- 1 small onion, quartered

Directions:

- Place a sheet of parchment paper on a baking sheet.
- Add spinach, almonds, cashews, oil, chia mixture, oats, salt and onions into the food processor bowl. Pulse until coarse in texture.
- Transfer into a bowl.
- Divide the mixture into 1-tablespoon portions and shape into balls.
- Place on the prepared baking sheet.
- Bake in a preheated oven 350° F for about 30 minutes or until light brown in color.
- Remove from the oven and cool for a while.
- Serve warm with a dip of your choice.

Lean Meatballs with Teriyaki Sauce

Sesame seeds are dense in nutrients. They are high in calcium and vitamin E. Honey is anti-inflammatory and anti-bacterial. It is anti-cancer.

Preparation time: 20 minutes

Number of servings: 8

Ingredients:

For teriyaki sauce:

- 4 tablespoons honey
- 5 tablespoons light soy sauce or tamari
- 4 tablespoons rice wine vinegar

For meatballs:

- 2 pounds lean ground beef or turkey
- 4 slices whole wheat bread, discard the sides
- 1 onion, minced
- 2 green onions, chopped, for garnishing
- ½ cup milk
- 2 tablespoons sesame seeds, toasted + extra for garnishing
- Salt to taste
- Pepper powder to taste
- 2 tablespoons sesame oil
- ¼ cup olive oil
- 2 eggs

Directions:

- To make teriyaki sauce: Mix together in a bowl, soy sauce, honey and rice wine vinegar and set aside.
- To make meatballs: Place bread slices in a bowl. Pour milk over it. Set aside for a few minutes and then squeeze the bread to drain off excess milk.
- Mix together in a large bowl the rest of the ingredients except olive oil. Add bread and mix well using your hands.
- Clean your hands and moisten if required.
- Make small balls of the mixture and set aside.
- Place a nonstick skillet over low heat and add 3 tablespoons of olive oil. When the oil is heated, add the meatballs and cook until brown on all the sides. Cook in batches if required.
- Add teriyaki sauce and mix well. Heat thoroughly.
- Garnish with green onions and sesame seeds. Insert toothpicks on the meatballs and serve immediately.

Quinoa Chia Seed Protein Bars

Quinoa suppresses the growth of cancer cells. They are high in protein and contain all the 9 essential amino acids. It is high in fiber, vitamin and minerals. Almonds are high in fiber and helps in building a strong immune system.

Preparation time: 5 minutes

Number of servings: 6

Ingredients:

- ¼ cup dry quinoa
- 1 tablespoon ground flax seeds
- A pinch Himalayan salt
- ½ teaspoon ground cardamom
- ½ teaspoon ground cinnamon
- 2 tablespoons honey
- ¼ cup almond butter
- ¼ cup chia seeds
- ½ cup rolled oats
- ¼ cup almonds, chopped
- 2 tablespoons brown rice syrup

Directions:

- Add almond butter, honey and brown rice syrup into a microwave safe bowl. Microwave on High for 40-50 seconds or until it melts. Mix well.

- Add quinoa, flaxseeds, salt, spices, chia seeds, oats and almonds into a bowl and stir.
- Transfer the almond butter mix into it. Mix well.
- Place rack in the middle of the oven
- Line a baking dish with butter paper. Transfer the mixture in the dish. Spread it evenly with a spatula.
- Bake in a preheated oven 350° F for about 15 minutes.
- Cool for 10-15 minutes. Remove the baked bar along with the parchment paper and cool on a wire rack.
- Cut into 6 equal squares and serve.

Chapter 6:
Lunch Recipes for Home

Sun-Dried Tomato and Broccoli Pizza

Tomatoes are super foods for fighting cancer. They are rich in vitamin A, C and E, which are necessary to fight cancer.

Preparation time: 15 minutes

Number of servings: 8-12

Ingredients:

- 2 store bought or homemade pizza crusts
- 6 ounces sun dried tomatoes or thinly sliced tomatoes as required
- 2 medium broccoli, cut into florets
- 4 cloves garlic, sliced
- 1 cup low fat feta cheese, crumbled
- 1 cup tomato basil pesto
- 15-16 black olives, pitted, sliced
- 1 ½ cups low fat mozzarella cheese, shredded
- ¼ cup pine nuts or slivered almonds, toasted

<u>For tomato basil pesto:</u>

- 2 cups tomatoes, peeled, deseeded, chopped
- 15-20 large basil leaves
- 2 teaspoons balsamic vinegar
- ½ cup parmesan cheese, freshly grated

- 3 cloves garlic, peeled
- ¼ cup extra virgin olive oil
- Salt to taste
- Freshly ground pepper to taste

Directions:

- To make tomato basil pesto: Add tomatoes, basil, vinegar, garlic, salt, pepper and oil into a blender.
- Blend for 30-40 seconds or until smooth.
- Add Parmesan cheese and pulse for 4-5 seconds until just combined. Use as much as required
- Transfer into a bowl. Cover and set aside for a while for the flavors to set in.
- To make pizza: If required, pour ¼ cup-boiling water over the sundried tomatoes. Let it soak for 10 minutes. Slice it thinly.
- Spread 7-8 tablespoons of the pesto over the crusts. Place sundried tomatoes, olives and broccoli all over the crusts. Sprinkle garlic and nuts. Sprinkle feta cheese and mozzarella cheese.
- Bake in a preheated oven 400° F for about 15-20 minutes depending on how crunchy or soft you like the pizza.
- Cut into wedges and serve.

Citrus Poached Salmon with Asparagus

Asparagus contains Asparanin A which stops the growth of liver cancer cells. It also contains the anti-oxidant glutathione, which is supposed to keep cancer away.

Preparation time: 5 minutes

Number of servings: 2

Ingredients:

- 2 salmon fillets (4 ounces each) fresh or frozen, rinsed, thawed if frozen
- Juice of ½ orange
- Juice of ½ lemon
- ½ teaspoon lemon zest, grated
- ½ pound asparagus spears, discard woody bases
- ½ cup water
- Pepper to taste
- Salt to taste
- 2 teaspoons melted butter
- A handful fresh parsley, snipped + extra to garnish

Directions:

- Dry the fish with paper towels or a clean kitchen towel.
- Set aside 2 tablespoons orange juice in a bowl and add the remaining juice into a skillet. Add water. Place the skillet over medium heat. Bring to the boil.

- Add salmon and lower heat to medium heat. Cover with a lid. Simmer for 4 minutes.
- Place asparagus over the salmon. Cover with a lid and simmer for 4-8 minutes until the fish flakes when pierced with a fork and the asparagus is crisp and tender as well.
- Add parsley, butter, lemon zest, salt and pepper into the bowl of orange juice that was set aside. Mix well.
- Place salmon and asparagus on a serving platter. Pour dressing on top. Sprinkle some more parsley leaves and serve.

Italian Veggie Salad

Radish, according to research arrests the growth of breast and stomach cancer. Radish has carotene, which is anti-cancerous.

Preparation time: 15 minutes

Number of servings: 4-6

Ingredients:

For the salad:

- 1 cup fresh baby carrots, quartered along the length
- 1 celery rib, sliced
- 3 large mushrooms, thinly sliced
- 2 cups cauliflower florets, cut into bite size florets
- 2 cups broccoli florets, cut into bite size florets
- 1 cup radish, thinly sliced
- 4-5 ounces hearts of romaine salad mix to serve

For dressing:

- ½ package Italian salad dressing mix
- 3 tablespoons white vinegar
- 3 tablespoons water
- 3 tablespoons olive oil
- 3-4 pepperoncini or to taste, chopped (optional)

Directions:

- Place a saucepan half filled with water over medium high heat. Bring to the boil.

- Add cauliflower and broccoli and bring to the boil. Let it boil for a minute.
- Transfer into a colander. Set aside to drain. Transfer into a large serving bowl. Let it cool.
- Add rest of the ingredients of the salad except hearts of romaine to the bowl of carrots and toss.
- To make dressing: Add Italian salad dressing mix, vinegar, water, oil and pepperoncini into a small glass jar. Close the lid and shake vigorously until well combined.
- Pour dressing over salad and toss well. Refrigerate for a couple of hours.
- Place romaine in a large bowl. Place the chilled salad over it. Toss well and serve.

Asian Salmon Lettuce Cups

Wild salmon has omega 3 fatty acids which are anti-inflammatory. It prevents cancer and stops the further growth of tumors.

Preparation time: 15 minutes

Number of servings: 6

Ingredients:

- 1 bunch Bibb lettuce leaves, separate the leaves
- 1 ½ cups white wine
- 3 teaspoons sesame oil, toasted
- 3 teaspoons fresh ginger, minced
- 3 tablespoons tamari or soy sauce
- 3 ounces water chestnuts
- 36 ounces wild salmon
- 3 medium scallions, thinly sliced

Directions:

- To poach salmon: Add wine and ¾ cup water into a large skillet.
- Place the skillet over medium heat. Bring to the boil.
- Lower heat and add salmon.
- Cover with a lid and let it cook until the salmon flakes readily with a fork.
- When cool enough to handle, remove the skin and chop the fish into 1-inch pieces.

- Add salmon into a bowl. Pour soy sauce and sesame oil and toss well. Sprinkle ginger and scallions on it. Add water chestnuts and toss well.
- Arrange the lettuce leaves on a serving platter. Divide the salmon mixture into the lettuce cups.
- Serve right away.

Creamy Mushroom Soup

Immunity is increased with the consumption of mushrooms. They arrest the growth of tumors. Cells are also regenerated.

Preparation time: 15 minutes

Number of servings: 3

Ingredients:

- ½ pound mushrooms, sliced
- 1 medium onion, chopped
- 1 medium potato, chopped
- 1 teaspoon olive oil
- 1 teaspoon sesame oil
- 2 cloves garlic, sliced
- Salt to taste
- 1 bay leaf
- Cayenne pepper to taste
- ½ cup chia seeds
- ½ teaspoon tamari or soy sauce or to taste
- ½ cup raw cashews
- 3 cups water

Directions:

- Add cashew and water into a blender and blend until smooth.
- Pour into a bowl. Add chia seeds and stir. Set aside for a while.

- Place a saucepan over low heat and add sesame oil. When the oil is heated, add half the mushrooms and sauté for 2-3 minutes. Transfer into the bowl of cashew milk.
- Place a saucepan over low heat and add olive oil. When the oil is heated, add bay leaf, onion, garlic and potato and sauté for a couple of minutes.
- Add a cup of water and stir. Bring to the boil.
- Lower heat and simmer until potato is tender.
- Add basil and tamari and stir. Add cashew milk. Bring to the boil. Turn off the heat. Discard the bay leaf. Cool for a while and blend with an immersion blender until smooth.
- Place the saucepan back over medium high heat. Add remaining mushrooms, salt and cayenne pepper. Simmer for 10-15 minutes.
- Ladle into soup bowls and serve.

Tomato and Lentil Soup

Lentils are fibrous and rich in phytochemicals, vitamins and minerals. Lentils are rich in the mineral selenium, which reduces inflammation.

Preparation time: 10 minutes

Number of servings: 2

Ingredients:

- 1 tablespoon olive oil
- 1 stick celery, sliced
- 2 cloves garlic, finely chopped
- 6 tablespoons red lentils, rinsed
- 3 large ripe tomatoes, chopped
- 1 tablespoon milled chia seeds
- 1 carrot, chopped
- 1 medium onion, chopped
- 2 ½ cups vegetable stock
- 1 can (15 ounces) plum tomatoes
- ½ small bunch fresh basil, chopped
- Salt to taste
- Pepper to taste

Directions:

- Place a saucepan over low heat and add oil. When the oil is heated, add onions and stir-fry them until the onions turn translucent.

- Then add carrots and celery and sauté for a couple of minutes.
- Add garlic and sauté for a few seconds until fragrant.
- Add stock and bring to the boil. Add lentils, tomatoes and canned tomatoes and stir. Let it boil.
- Lower heat and cover with a lid. Simmer until lentils are tender.
- Turn off heat. Add basil and stir.
- Blend it in a mixer until smooth.
- Add salt and pepper.
- Ladle into soup bowls and serve.

Chapter 7: Lunch Recipes for Work

Kale Turkey Wraps

Kale tops the list of anti-cancerous foods. It prevents the turning of tumors into cancer. Kale increases immunity. Pears are anti-oxidants and high in fiber. This helps in fighting free radicles and detoxifying the body.

Preparation time: 10 minutes

Number of servings: 2 (3 wraps each)

Ingredients:

- 2 tablespoons cranberry sauce
- 6 medium lacinato kale leaves or cabbage leaves
- 12 thin slices red onion
- 2 teaspoons Dijon mustard
- 6 slices deli turkey
- 2 firm ripe pears, cut each into 9 slices each

Directions:

- Add mustard and cranberry sauce into a bowl and stir.
- Spread the leaves on your countertop. Spread the sauce mixture on the leaves.
- Place a slice of turkey on each leaf. Place 2 slices onion and 3 slices pears over the turkey on each leaf.
- Wrap and place with the seam side down in your lunch box.

Crunch-Time Veggie Wrap

Avocadoes are rich in carotenoids that help in fighting against cancer. It has a type of fat called avocatin B which helps fight acute myeloid leukemia.

Preparation time: minutes

Number of servings: 2

Ingredients:

- 2 light whole wheat flatbreads or whole wheat tortillas
- 1 teaspoon lime juice
- ½ small cucumber, cut into matchsticks
- ½ medium avocado, peeled, pitted, sliced
- 2 medium carrots, cut into matchsticks
- 2 tablespoons feta cheese, crumbled
- ½ small red bell pepper, deseeded, cut into matchsticks

Directions:

- Add avocado into a bowl and mash it well. Add lime juice and stir.
- Place the flat breads on a serving platter. Spread the avocado mixture over the flat breads.
- Place the carrot, cucumber and red peppers over the breads. Top with feta cheese.
- Wrap and cover with plastic wrap. Place in your lunch box.

Tomato, Smoked Salmon, and Arugula Stacks

Arugula is high in phytochemicals; vitamin A, vitamin B, vitamin C and vitamin K. Arugula contains glucosinolates which helps fight cancer.

Preparation time: 10 minutes

Number of servings: 2

Ingredients:

For dressing:

- ½ teaspoon Dijon mustard
- 2 teaspoons extra virgin olive oil
- ½ tablespoon white wine vinegar

For salad:

- 1 small red onion, thinly sliced
- 4 ounces smoked salmon, cut into 8 portions
- 2 cups arugula leaves
- 4 small tomatoes, halved crosswise
- 2 slices mozzarella cheese or provolone cheese (optional)

Directions:

- To make dressing: add mustard and vinegar into a bowl. Whisk well.
- Add olive oil in a thin stream whisking simultaneously.

- Take 2 wide mason's jars.
- Place 2 tomato halves in each jar, next to each other. Place a salmon piece over each tomato. Top with arugula. Tear the cheese slice and place over the arugula. Divide and pour the dressing on top.
- Fasten the lid and carry to your work place.

Buffalo Chicken Wraps

Chicken has choline, selenium, vitamin D, zinc, iron and vitamin B6 apart from other nutrition. Butter lettuce is high in vitamin K.

Preparation time: 8 minutes

Number of servings: 2

Ingredients:

- 1 tablespoon butter
- 1 small green bell pepper, diced
- 1 small red bell pepper, diced
- 2 stalks celery, diced
- 1 teaspoon onion powder
- ¼ cup Frank's Red hot sauce (optional)
- 1 scallion, sliced
- Salt to taste
- Pepper to taste
- 1 pound chicken thighs, skinless, boneless, cut into bite size pieces
- ½ teaspoon garlic powder
- ¼ cup blue cheese, crumbled
- ½ head butter lettuce, separate the leaves (4-5 leaves)

Directions:

- Place a skillet over low heat and add butter. When butter melts, add both the bell peppers and celery and cook until the vegetables are slightly tender.

- Add chicken, garlic and onion powders and sauté for a couple of minutes.
- Add salt and pepper and cook until chicken is tender.
- Add hot sauce and stir for a couple of minutes. The chicken should be well coated with the sauce.
- Turn off the heat. Stir in the blue cheese and scallions.
- Place the lettuce leaves on a serving platter. Divide the mixture among the lettuce leaves. Wrap and pack in your lunch box.
- You can also use tortillas or flat bread to wrap the chicken.

Broccoli Sprouts and Arugula Salad with Blackberries, Papaya and Almonds

Papaya is full of anti-oxidants. It contains choline and beta-carotene, which fights cancer. Blackberries are anti-oxidants and are anti-inflammatory too.

Preparation time: 10 minutes

Number of servings: 2

Ingredients:

- 2 tablespoons fresh grapefruit juice
- 1 tablespoon flaxseed oil
- Salt to taste
- Pepper to taste
- 3 cup arugula
- ¼ cup almonds, chopped
- 1 tablespoon all-fruit blackberry preserve
- ½ tablespoon extra-virgin olive oil
- 2 ounces broccoli sprouts
- ½ cup papaya cubes
- ½ cup blackberries, fresh or frozen, thaw if frozen

Directions:

- Add grapefruit juice, flaxseed oil, blackberry preserve and olive oil into a bowl. Whisk well. Add salt and pepper and whisk well.

- Add broccoli sprouts, papaya, arugula and almonds into a bowl. Pour the dressing on it. Toss well.
- Divide the arugula salad among 2 wide mason's jars. Pour dressing on top.
- Divide the blackberries among the jars.
- Fasten the lid and carry to your work place.

Southwestern Salad with Black Beans

Black beans contain selenium, which is an anti-inflammatory. It also contains saponins, which prevents the increase of cancer cells in the body and stops it from spreading.

Preparation time: 15 minutes

Number of servings: 2

Ingredients:

- 1 ripe avocado, peeled, pitted, chopped
- 1 cup nonfat plain yogurt
- 2 cloves garlic, quartered
- ¼ teaspoon sugar
- 6 cups mixed greens
- 1 cup corn kernels, fresh or frozen, thaw if frozen
- 1 ½ cups fresh cilantro
- 4 scallions, chopped
- 2 tablespoons lime juice
- 1 teaspoon salt
- 1 cup cooked or canned black beans
- 1 cup grape tomatoes

Directions:

- Add avocado, yogurt, lime juice, sugar, salt, cilantro, garlic and scallions into a blender and blend until smooth.
- Divide the greens among 2 mason's jars.
- Place black beans, tomatoes and corn over it.

- Drizzle the dressing over it. Use as much as required and store the remaining dressing in the refrigerator for another use.
- Close the lid and carry to your work place.

Chapter 8:
Anti-cancer Dinner Recipes

Spanish Spinach with Chickpeas (Garbanzos con espinacas)

Spinach contains carotenoids that help fight free radicals. Chickpeas are high in fiber and iron.

Preparation time: 5 minutes

Number of servings: 2

Ingredients:

- 2 teaspoons extra virgin olive oil
- 1 ½ tablespoons sweet paprika
- ¼ cup water or more if required
- Sea salt to taste
- 1 ¾ cups cooked chickpeas
- 6 cloves garlic, chopped
- 3 cups spinach, finely chopped

<u>For toasted baguette:</u>

- 4 slices whole wheat baguette
- Olive oil to drizzle
- Pimento to sprinkle

Directions:

- Place a skillet over low heat and add oil. When the oil is heated, add garlic and sauté until golden brown.
- Add spinach and paprika and mix well. Add water and salt and cook until spinach wilts.
- Add chickpeas and a little more olive oil if desired and bring to the boil.
- Turn off heat and serve with toasted baguette.
- To make toasted baguette: Place the baguettes on a baking sheet. Drizzle oil over it. Sprinkle pimento on top.
- Bake in a preheated oven at 350° F for 10 minutes or until toasted as per your desire.

Caraway Chicken and Vegetable Stew with Garlic Bread

Celery, mushrooms and carrots are high in anti-oxidants. Celery is rich in vitamin C, K and potassium, which lower the risk of cancer.

Preparation time: 15 minutes

Number of servings: 3

Ingredients:

- 1 ½ pounds chicken thighs and / or bone-in breasts, skinless
- 1 teaspoon instant chicken bouillon granules
- ½ teaspoon caraway seeds, crushed
- 4 ounces fresh green beans, trimmed, cut into 2 inch pieces
- 1 stalk celery, cut into 2 inch pieces
- ½ cup pearl onions, peeled
- 2 cups water
- ½ teaspoon salt or to taste
- Pepper to taste
- 1 medium carrot, peeled, chopped into ¾ inch chunks
- 1 cup shiitake or button mushrooms, sliced
- 2 tablespoons all-purpose flour mixed with 2 tablespoons water

For garlic bread:

- 3 tablespoons butter

- 1 teaspoon dried parsley
- ½ loaf whole wheat Italian bread, cut into ½ inch thick slices
- 1 teaspoon garlic powder
- 3 ounces mozzarella cheese, shredded

Directions:

- Place a Dutch oven over low heat and add water, chicken, bouillon granules, salt, pepper and caraway seeds into it. Bring to the boil.
- Lower heat and cover with a lid. Simmer for 20-25 minutes.
- Add all the vegetables and cover with a lid. Simmer until chicken is tender.
- Remove the chicken pieces with a slotted spoon and place on your cutting board. When cool enough to handle, discard the bones and chop the chicken into smaller pieces.
- Add chicken back into the Dutch oven. Let it simmer.
- Add all-purpose flour mixture and stir constantly until thick. Simmer for a couple of minutes.
- Ladle into soup bowls and serve with garlic bread.
- Make garlic bread as follows: Place a small saucepan over low heat and add butter. When butter melts, turn off heat. Add garlic powder and parsley and stir until well combined.
- Lay the bread slices on a baking sheet. Brush the garlic butter mixture liberally over the bread slices.
- Bake in a preheated oven at 350° F for 10 minutes or until toasted as per your desire.

- Remove the baking sheet from the oven and top with mozzarella cheese. Drizzle the remaining butter mixture if any and bake for another 5 minutes.

Curried Spring Vegetable Sauté with Tempeh and Garlic Roasted Chicken

Turmeric also helps in reducing the pain associated with arthritis. It also helps fight certain types of cancers. Cabbage is rich in vitamin K1, anti-oxidants and glucosinolates. It is an anti-inflammatory too. These are very necessary to fight cancer. Tempeh is highly beneficial in preventing cancer.

Preparation time: 20 minutes

Number of servings: 3

Ingredients:

For curried spring vegetable sauté:

- ½ tablespoon unrefined coconut oil
- ½ tablespoon fresh ginger, minced
- 1 medium yellow onion, chopped
- 2 cloves garlic, minced
- ½ fennel bulb, sliced
- ¼ pound sugar snap peas
- ½ tablespoon fresh ginger, minced
- 2 cups cabbage, thinly sliced
- 2 carrots, sliced
- 1 teaspoon ground cumin
- 1 teaspoon ground coriander
- 1 teaspoon ground turmeric or 2 teaspoons fresh turmeric, minced
- Cayenne pepper to taste (optional)

- 1 cup low sodium vegetable broth
- ¼ teaspoon ground mustard
- 4 ounces tempeh, cut into small pieces
- Salt to taste (optional)

For garlic roasted chicken:

- 2 large cloves garlic, peeled, minced
- ½ teaspoon red pepper flakes
- 3 chicken breast halves with skin and bones
- ¾ teaspoon dried oregano
- 4 teaspoons extra virgin olive oil
- 1 teaspoon salt
- ½ teaspoon pepper powder

Directions:

- To make garlic roasted chicken: Add salt to garlic and mash it well. Add oregano, red pepper flakes, olive oil and pepper and mix well.
- Make a slit like a pocket in each of the chicken pieces horizontally. It should be around 1 ½ inches deep. Smear ½ teaspoon garlic mixture inside the pockets.
- Smear the chicken with the remaining garlic mixture.
- Line a baking dish with aluminum foil. Place the chicken in it with the skin side facing up.
- Place rack in the oven in the upper third part of the oven.
- Place the baking dish on the rack.
- Roast in a preheated oven at 500° F for 20-25 minutes or until cooked. As it is roasting, make the vegetable sauté.

- To make curried vegetable sauté: Place a skillet over low heat and add oil. When the oil is heated, add onion, garlic and ginger and sauté until onions turns lightly brown.
- Add all the vegetables and sauté for a couple of minutes. Add turmeric and sauté for 10-15 seconds. Add mustard and rest of the spices and sauté for 5-10 seconds.
- Add tempeh and broth. Bring to the boil.
- Lower heat and cover with a lid. Simmer until vegetables are soft as per your liking.
- Taste and adjust the seasonings if necessary. Serve with Garlic roasted chicken breasts

Ma'aluba

Cauliflower is rich in protein and contains sulpforaphane which helps in killing cancer cells and thereby slows the growth of tumors. It is an anti-inflammatory and boosts heart health.

Preparation time: 20 minutes

Number of servings: 3

Ingredients:

- 3 small onions, sliced
- A pinch saffron threads
- ½ teaspoon dried thyme
- Freshly ground pepper to taste
- 3 small potatoes, sliced
- 1 small eggplant, quartered, cut into ½ inch thick slices
- 1 cup cauliflower florets
- Paprika to taste
- 1 ¾ cups vegetable broth
- 1 ½ tablespoons extra virgin olive oil + extra to brush
- ½ tablespoon turmeric powder
- ½ teaspoon nutmeg, ground or grated
- Sea salt to taste
- 3 chicken breasts, skinless
- 1 ¼ cups brown basmati rice, uncooked, rinsed

Directions:

- Place a large nonstick skillet over low heat and add ½ tablespoon oil. When the oil is heated, add onions and sauté until golden brown.
- Stir in 1-teaspoon turmeric, nutmeg, thyme, saffron and pepper. Sauté for a few seconds until fragrant. Remove the onions with a slotted spoon and set aside.
- Add ½ tablespoon oil. When the oil is heated, add potatoes and sauté until golden brown on both the sides. It should not be cooked inside, only golden brown on the sides. Remove the potatoes with a slotted spoon and set aside.
- Add ½ tablespoon oil. When the oil is heated, add cauliflower and cook until golden brown. Remove the cauliflower with a slotted spoon and set aside.
- Add eggplant and sauté until light brown. Remove with a slotted spoon and set aside.
- Brush a little olive oil all over the chicken. Sprinkle paprika and turmeric all over it.
- Spread the onions at the bottom of a Dutch oven. Place chicken over it. Stuff in the eggplant between the chicken. Spread cauliflower over the chicken and the potatoes over the cauliflower.
- Layer with rice. Pour broth.
- Do not cover the Dutch oven and place it over medium heat. Let it cook for 8-9 minutes.
- Cover the Dutch oven now.

- Lower heat to low heat and cook for 25-30 minutes or until rice is tender. Add more broth if you find that the rice is uncooked. Add a little at a time so that it does not get overcooked.
- When the meal is cooked and ready, it will smell slightly burnt. Turn off the heat.
- Place a large round metal tray or serving platter over the top of the pot and invert the pot on to the tray. Tap a little if necessary to drop the onions and chicken.
- Serve right away.

Chicken with Brussels sprouts and Mustard Sauce and Rosemary Potatoes

Brussels sprouts protect against free radical damage. They contain sulforaphane, which is a sulphur-containing compound; it helps fight against cancer. They also contain other compounds that protect against cancer.

Preparation time: 20 minutes

Number of servings: 2

Ingredients:

- 1 tablespoon olive oil, divided
- Salt to taste
- 6 tablespoons low sodium chicken broth, divided
- 1 tablespoon whole grain Dijon mustard
- A handful fresh flat leaf parsley, chopped
- 2 chicken breast halves (6 ounces each), skinless, boneless
- Freshly ground pepper to taste
- 2 tablespoons unfiltered apple cider vinegar
- 1 tablespoon butter, divided
- 6 ounces Brussels sprouts, trimmed, halved

<u>For rosemary potatoes:</u>

- ¾ pound small red or white skinned potatoes, halved or quartered
- ¼ teaspoon freshly ground pepper
- 1 tablespoon fresh rosemary leaves, minced

- 1-2 tablespoons olive oil
- Kosher salt to taste
- ½ tablespoon garlic, minced

Directions:

- To make chicken with Brussels sprouts: Place an ovenproof skillet over high heat. Add ½ tablespoon oil and let it heat.
- Season chicken with salt and pepper and place in the skillet. Cook until the underside is golden brown. Flip sides and remove from heat.
- Place the skillet in a preheated oven.
- Bake in a preheated oven at 450° F for 8-9 minutes or until tender.
- Remove the chicken from the oven and pan and keep warm.
- Place the skillet back over heat. Pour broth and cider vinegar and bring to the boil. Scrape the bottom of the pan to remove any bits that may be stuck.
- Lower heat and simmer for 3-4 minutes. Add mustard, ½ tablespoon butter and parsley and stir. Turn off the heat.
- Place a nonstick skillet over low heat and add ½ tablespoon oil and ½ tablespoon butter. When butter melts, add Brussels sprouts and stir-fry for a couple of minutes until light brown.
- Season with salt. Pour remaining broth and stir. Cover with a lid.
- Cook for 3-4 minutes until the broth dries up.

- Meanwhile make the roasted potatoes: Add potatoes into a bowl. Sprinkle salt, pepper, rosemary and garlic. Toss well. Drizzle oil and toss well.
- Spread it on a baking sheet in a single layer.
- Bake in a preheated oven at 400° F until tender. Turn the potatoes a couple of times while it is baking.
- Serve chicken with mustard sauce and Brussels sprouts along with rosemary-roasted potatoes.

Punjabi-spiced Scottish Salmon

Salmon is high in omega 3 fatty acid, protein, vitamin B, selenium, potassium, etc. It contains astaxanthin, which is a powerful anti-oxidant.

Preparation time: minutes

Number of servings: 2

Ingredients:

- ½ cup tomatoes, chopped
- 2 small chili peppers, finely chopped
- ½ teaspoon ground cumin
- ½ teaspoon turmeric powder
- ¼ teaspoon mustard seeds
- ¼ teaspoon garam masala
- 2 salmon fillets (6 ounces each)
- Olive oil, as required
- ½ teaspoon salt or to taste
- ½ teaspoon carom seeds
- 2 cloves garlic, finely chopped
- 2 ½ tablespoons fresh ginger, peeled, finely chopped
- ¾ cup leeks, slivered
- Cooked basmati rice to serve

For tomato garnish:

- 1 clove garlic, chopped
- ½ cup yellow cherry tomatoes
- ½ cup red cherry tomatoes
- 2 tablespoons fresh thyme leaves, chopped

- 2 tablespoons fresh tarragon leaves, chopped
- 1 bay leaf, crumbled
- Salt to taste
- Pepper to taste
- Sugar to taste

Directions:

- For Punjabi spiced Scottish salmon: Add tomatoes, garlic, ginger, turmeric powder, chili pepper, cumin, mustard seeds, garam masala and salt into a bowl toss well.
- Add salmon and toss until well coated. Marinate for 2-6 hours.
- Place a small pan over low heat and add a little oil. When the oil is heated, add leeks and cook until crisp. Remove with a slotted spoon and place on a plate that is lined with paper towels.
- Sprinkle salt and pepper over it and set aside.
- To make tomato garnish: Grease a rimmed baking sheet with oil. Sprinkle salt, pepper, garlic and sugar all over the baking sheet.
- Spread the tomatoes over it. Sprinkle thyme leaves and tarragon leaves. Toss well.
- Bake in a preheated oven at 400° F until a few blisters appear on the tomatoes. Remove the tomatoes from the oven and keep warm.
- To make salmon: Place a pan over low heat and add a little olive oil. Let it heat. When it begins to smoke, turn off heat. After a minute, add carom seeds.

- Place it back on heat after a minute. Immediately add salmon along with the marinade.
- Turn off the heat when the salmon is nearly cooked but not fully cooked.
- Place basmati rice in the center of the plate. Surround the rice with tomatoes.
- Place salmon over the rice. Garnish with fried leeks and serve.

Sweet Potato Tofu Curry with Mushroom Brown Rice Pilaf

Dark colored sweet potatoes are higher in nutrition than lighter colored ones. Sweet potatoes are loaded with phytochemicals and carotenoids. They have high protein content called sporamin that slows the growth of cancer cells.

Preparation time: 25 minutes

Number of servings: 6

Ingredients:

For sweet potato tofu curry:

- 2 large sweet potatoes, peeled, cubed
- 2 yellow onions, finely chopped
- 28 ounces tofu, drained, cubed
- 4 tablespoons coconut oil or any oil of your choice
- 1 tablespoon ginger paste
- 1 tablespoon garlic paste
- 1 red bell pepper, cut into 1 inch cubes
- 1 yellow bell pepper, cut into 1 inch cubes
- 1 green bell pepper, cut into 1 inch cubes
- 1 orange bell pepper, cut into 1 inch cubes
- 2 cups green beans, cut into 2 inch pieces
- 6 green chilies, ground into a chunky paste
- 2 cans coconut milk
- 2 cans water
- 15-20 curry leaves
- 1 teaspoon ground cumin

- 2 teaspoons ground turmeric
- Salt to taste

For mushroom brown rice pilaf:

- 4 tablespoons extra virgin olive oil
- 8 medium scallions, thinly sliced crosswise
- 6 large cloves garlic, coarsely chopped
- 1 ½ cups long grain brown rice
- 1 ½ cups water
- 1 ½ cups vegetable stock or broth
- ½ lime
- ¾ pound small white mushrooms, quartered
- Salt to taste
- Freshly ground pepper to taste
- 1 ½ tablespoons soy sauce or to taste (optional)

To serve:

- 1 cup peanuts, roasted
- ¼ teaspoon red chili flakes
- 4 green onions, thinly sliced

Directions:

- To make mushroom brown rice pilaf: Place a skillet over low heat and add 4 tablespoons olive oil. When the oil is heated, add most of the scallions, mushrooms, salt and pepper and sauté until all the released liquid in the pan dry up.
- Add remaining oil and garlic. Raise the heat to high heat. Sauté until garlic is golden brown.

- Add soy sauce, rice, water and broth and stir. Bring to the boil. Turn off the heat.
- Transfer into a large glass-baking dish.
- Cover the dish with foil.
- Bake in a preheated oven at 350° F until the rice is cooked and all the liquid is absorbed. It should take 45-60 minutes.
- When done, remove from the oven. Sprinkle the retained scallions and fluff rice with a fork. Meanwhile, as the rice is being cooked, make the curry.
- To make sweet potato tofu curry: Place a large wok over low heat and add oil. When the oil is heated, onions and sauté until translucent.
- Add green chili paste, ginger paste, garlic paste, turmeric and ground cumin and sauté until light brown.
- Add sweet potatoes and sauté for 4-5 minutes. Stir frequently. Sprinkle water if you think the mixture is getting stuck to the wok or is burning.
- Add beans and bell peppers and sauté for 4-5 minutes.
- Add tofu, coconut milk, water, salt and tofu. Stir well.
- Cover with a lid and cook until the sweet potatoes are tender. Taste and adjust the seasoning if necessary.
- Place cooked brown rice pilaf on individual serving plates. Pour the curry over it. Sprinkle peanuts, chili flakes, and green onions on top and serve.

Peanut Butter Rice with Cruciferous Vegetables

Cruciferous vegetables are high in fiber and contain anti-oxidants like beta-carotene. It has tons of vitamin C, E and K. These vegetables protect the cells from DNA damage. They make the carcinogens inactive.

Preparation time: 20 minutes

Number of servings: 6

Ingredients:

- 2 cups long brown rice, rinsed, drained
- 1 large head cauliflower, chopped into florets
- ½ cup green onions, chopped
- 1 large head red cabbage, thinly sliced
- 2 packages firm tofu, chopped into bite size cubes or cooked chicken strips
- 4 cups water
- 4 tablespoons coconut oil, divided
- 2 teaspoons Himalayan pink salt, divided
- ½ cup fresh cilantro, chopped
- 2-3 tablespoons roasted peanuts

For peanut butter sauce:

- 1 cup peanut butter, unsalted
- 2 cups mango chunks, fresh or frozen
- 1 cup warm water
- 4 large cloves garlic, minced

- ½ cup soy sauce
- 2 inches ginger, peeled, minced

Directions:

- Place a pot over low heat and add water and rice and bring to the boil.
- Lower heat and cover with a lid. Cook until the rice is tender.
- Meanwhile, add all the ingredients of the peanut butter sauce into a blender and blend until smooth. Transfer into a bowl and set aside.
- Place a large wok over low heat and add 2 tablespoons coconut oil. When the oil is melted, add cabbage and salt and sauté for a few minutes until the cabbage begins to char. Cook for longer if you like it more charred.
- Transfer on to a plate.
- Pour the remaining oil into the wok. Add cauliflower and salt and sauté until tender.
- Add the cooked rice and cabbage into the wok and stir. Remove from heat.
- Add tofu or chicken and stir.
- Sprinkle peanuts and green onions. Drizzle the peanut butter sauce and stir until well combined.
- Serve either hot or warm.

Chapter 9:
Anti-cancer Dessert Recipes

Green Tea-Poached Asian Pears with Pistachio Cream Sauce

Green tea contains the highest amount of catechins. Green tea prevents the formation of cancer in liver, breast, colon etc. The anti-oxidants found in green tea stop the growing of cancer cells.

Preparation time: 10 minutes

Number of servings: 8

Ingredients:

- 8 Asian pears, unblemished, peeled, cored
- 4 cups hot water
- 4 green tea bags
- Zest of a lemon, grated
- Fresh mint leaves, to garnish
- 2 cups natural brown sugar (turbinado sugar)
- 4 inch piece fresh ginger, peeled, sliced into thin rounds
- 2 large sprigs fresh mint

For pistachio cream sauce:

- 2 cups nonfat plain yogurt, drained

- 2 tablespoons pure maple syrup
- 1 cup buttermilk
- 1 cup shelled, skinned, natural pistachios, coarsely chopped

Directions:

- Drop the tea bags in hot water. Let it brew for 2-3 minutes. Discard the bags.
- Add green tea, lemon zest, ginger slices and mint sprigs in a large saucepan.
- Place the saucepan over medium heat. Bring to the boil.
- Lower heat and place the pears in the pan. Let it simmer for 15-20 minutes. They should be firm and not over cooked.
- Turn off the heat and cool completely. Cover with a lid. Refrigerate until use.
- To make pistachio cream sauce: Add buttermilk, yogurt and maple syrup into a bowl and whisk well. Add pistachio nuts and stir. Refrigerate until use. Also chill 8 goblets until use.
- To serve: Drain the cooked liquid. Place a pear in each goblet.
- Drizzle sauce over the pears. Garnish with mint and serve.

Fresh Berry Cups

In particular blueberries and raspberries help in preventing cancer. Blueberries contain pterostilbene, which is an anti-oxidant that fights cancer. All types of berries are high in vitamin C.

Preparation time: 10 minutes

Number of servings: 6

Ingredients:

- 3 ½ cups mixed berries (mixture of strawberries, blueberries, blackberries and raspberries)
- 2 tablespoons brown rice syrup
- Organic canola oil cooking spray
- 2 tablespoons natural cane sugar
- 3 ½ tablespoons Chambord crème de cassis (blackcurrant liqueur)
- 4 sheets phyllo pastry, thawed
- 2 tablespoons water
- ½ tablespoon arrowroot powder

Directions:

- Add 2 cups berries into a bowl. Pour 2 tablespoons liqueur and brown rice syrup over it. Mix well. Set aside.
- Place a phyllo sheet on your countertop. Place remaining sheets on a damp towel. Cover with another damp towel.

- Spray the phyllo sheet on your countertop with cooking spray.
- Carefully pick another phyllo sheet (from between the towels) and place over this sheet.
- Repeat the above step twice more. In all you have 4 phyllo sheets in a stack.
- Chop the phyllo sheet layers into 6 equal squares.
- Grease 6 muffin cups with cooking spray.
- Carefully lift the chopped squares and fit one in each muffin cup.
- Bake in a preheated oven at 350° F for 5-7 minutes or until golden brown.
- Meanwhile, add remaining berries into a saucepan. Add 2 tablespoons water. Place the saucepan over medium heat. Cook until a thick sauce is obtained.
- Pass the mixture through a fine wire mesh strainer, which is placed over a bowl. Press the mixture to get as much liquid as possible. Discard the squeezed out berries.
- Pour the juice back into the saucepan. Stir in 1 ½ tablespoons liqueur and sugar.
- Place the saucepan over medium heat. Stir frequently until the sugar dissolves.
- Take a tablespoon of the sauce and add into a bowl. Let it cool slightly. Add arrowroot powder and whisk until well combined.
- Pour the arrowroot powder into the saucepan and stir constantly until the mixture thickens. Taste and adjust the sweetness if required. Turn off the heat.
- Spoon the berries (soaked in liqueur) into the phyllo cups.

- Drizzle some of the berry sauce on the center of 6 dessert plates. Place a berry filled cup on each and serve with extra sauce if desired.

Rainbow Sundae

Apples contain phytonutrients and anti-oxidants that are essential to combat cancer. Kiwi has an abundance of vitamin C and vitamin E, which are powerful anti-oxidants. It is an anti-inflammatory. All the fruits used in this recipe are high in vitamin C and are powerful anti-oxidants.

Preparation time: 10 minutes

Number of servings: 12

Ingredients:

- 2 ripe bananas, sliced, frozen
- 1-2 apples or pears, peeled, cored, chopped
- 2/3 cup pineapple pieces
- 1 kiwi, chopped
- 1 cup purple grapes, seedless
- ½ cup blackberries or raspberries
- 4 strawberries, chopped
- 1-2 oranges, peeled, separated into segments, deseeded
- 4 dates, pitted, chopped
- ¼ cup nuts of your choice
- 1/3 cup boiling water
- ¼ cup almond milk
- ¼ teaspoon ground ginger
- ½ tablespoon almond butter, unsweetened
- 1 cup granola of your choice
- 2 tablespoons chia seeds

Directions:

- Soak dates in boiling water for at least 45 minutes. Drain the dates.
- Add dates and ginger into a blender. Also add a little water and blend into a smooth sauce and keep it aside.
- Clean the blender and blend together the frozen bananas, almond butter and almond milk. Transfer into 12 freezer safe dessert bowls and freeze until firm.
- Remove from the freezer and sprinkle pineapple, kiwi, strawberry, grapes, blackberries, orange and apple or pears over it.
- Sprinkle granola, nuts and chia seeds. Pour date sauce on top and serve.

Antioxidant Muffins

Whole wheat has lot of fiber. It is very helpful against breast cancer. It is an anti-inflammatory too. Pecans help fight breast cancer as they contain a fatty acid called oleic acid. It also prevents colon cancer.

Preparation time: 10 minutes

Number of servings: 12-15

Ingredients:

- 2 cups whole wheat flour
- ½ teaspoon salt
- ½ cup almond milk
- 1 teaspoon baking powder
- 2/3 cup brown sugar
- 2/3 cup pecans, chopped
- 2 cups blueberries
- 2 large eggs

Directions:

- Add whole-wheat flour, baking powder, salt, sugar and pecans into a bowl and mix well.
- Add eggs into another bowl. Beat lightly. Add almond milk and beat again.
- Pour the egg mixture into the bowl of flour mixture. Whisk well.

- Add blueberries and fold gently.
- Line 12-15 muffin cups with disposable liners. Spoon the batter in the cups. Fill up to 2/3.
- Bake in a preheated oven at 350° F for 25-30 minutes or until a toothpick comes clean, when injected in the center of the muffin
- Take it out of the oven and cool.
- Serve warm or at room temperature.

Creamy Chocolate-Avocado Ice Cream

Almond milk contains lots of protein and fiber. It contains vitamin C, E and vitamin B6 and many more minerals like calcium, iron, zinc, folate etc. the list is endless.

Preparation time: 15 minutes

Number of servings: 10-12

Ingredients:

- 27 ounces almond milk (or coconut milk if desired)
- 1 cup cocoa powder, unsweetened
- 2 tablespoons vanilla extract
- Hot chocolate fudge sauce to drizzle, as required
- 9 ounces chopped avocado
- 1 ¼ cups maple syrup
- 1 cup water
- Chopped walnuts or roasted, chopped almonds to sprinkle

For chocolate fudge sauce:

- 2/3 cup pitted dates (measure after pitting)
- 2 ounces unsweetened baking chocolate, grated

- 1 cup almond milk or any other milk of your choice

Directions:

- Blend together avocado and coconut milk until smooth.
- Add rest of the ingredients and blend until smooth.
- Pour into an ice cream maker and churn following to the manufacturer's instructions manual.
- Transfer into a freezer safe container.
- Cover and freeze until set.
- Alternately, pour the mixture into a freezer safe container and freeze. After about an hour of freezing, remove the ice cream from the freezer and whisk well. Refreeze and beat again after 30-40 minutes.
- Repeat the above step a couple of times more until well frozen without ice crystals.
- To make chocolate fudge sauce: If the dates are not soft, soak in hot water for 30 minutes. Drain and use. Add almond milk and dates into a blender and blend until smooth.

- Transfer into a saucepan. Place the saucepan over medium heat. Bring to the boil. Stir frequently.
- Lower heat and simmer until thick. Turn off heat and add chocolate. Let it sit for a minute. Whisk until chocolate melts in it. Use as required. Unused sauce should be transferred into a jar and refrigerated until use.
- To serve: Scoop ice cream into bowls. Drizzle hot fudge on top. Sprinkle the nuts on top and serve.

Brown Rice Porridge with Roasted Blueberries

Brown rice is high in fiber, selenium and magnesium which helps fight specially against colon cancer. Sprouted brown rice is even more nutritious than brown rice and oozing with a whole lot of vitamins and minerals. Honey prevents inflammation and is an anti-bacterial.

Preparation time: 10 minutes

Number of servings: 8

Ingredients:

For porridge:

- 2 cups sprouted brown rice, rinsed in cold water
- 2 teaspoons vanilla extract
- 7 cups almond milk
- A large pinch sea salt
- Honey to taste (optional)

For roasted blueberries:

- 6 cups blueberries
- Juice of a lemon
- 4 tablespoons honey or to taste
- A pinch sea salt

Directions:

- Place a heavy bottomed saucepan over medium high heat. Add rice, milk, salt and vanilla and bring to the boil. Stir occasionally.
- Lower heat and simmer until the rice is very soft and looks like pudding. It should take 45-60 minutes. Stir every 10 minutes or so.
- Meanwhile, roast the blueberries as follows: Add blueberries into a bowl. Drizzle honey and lemon juice over it. Sprinkle salt and toss until well combined.
- Bake in a preheated oven at 350° F for about 15 minutes or until the juices are released.
- Serve porridge in serving bowls. Drizzle a little honey. Place roasted blueberries on top and serve.

Chapter 10: Anti-cancer Kale Recipes

Kale and Mozzarella Scrambled Eggs

Makes 2 servings

You can substitute any type of cheese for the mozzarella if you prefer and, if inclined, you can select any herb combination that suits your taste.

Ingredients

- 1 cup of finely sliced Kale with the stems removed
- 4 large fresh Eggs, lightly beaten
- ½ cup of Mozzarella Cheese or your own choice
- ¼ cup of finely diced Onion
- ½ tsp of Italian Seasoning
- A medium pinch of Red Chili Powder
- 1 tsp of Coconut Oil or Ghee
- Sea Salt and freshly cracked Black Pepper

Directions

1. Sautee the onion in a heavy bottomed pan on a high heat with the oil and chili powder
2. Add the kale to the pan and continue sautéing until it's wilted
3. Turn the heat to medium low and add the beaten eggs. Stirring until they start to set, then stir in the cheese. Stir until all is well combined and season with salt and pepper, then serve.

Kale and Sweet Potato Fritters

Makes 18 to 20 mini patties or serving for 4 people

With a crispy exterior and soft, creamy interior, these tasty little fritters are full of vitamins and flavor, a breakfast treat with a spicy dip and your style of eggs, making a filling breakfast

Ingredients

- 2 cups of finely sliced Kale with stalks removed
- 3 cups of pureed, steamed, Sweet Potato
- 2 cups of cooked Quinoa
- 2 fresh Eggs
- 3 tbsp of Cornstarch
- ½ a cup of Bread Crumbs or Ground Oats
- 1 tsp of grated Ginger
- ¼ of a tsp of Smoked Paprika, ground
- 1 tsp of freshly cracked Black Pepper
- 1 tsp Of Sea Salt
- ¼ of a cup of Coconut Oil or Ghee

For the Dipping Sauce

- ¼ of a cup of Yogurt

- 1 tsp of freshly grated Ginger
- 2 tbsp of Chili Sauce
- Sea Salt and Cracked Black Pepper to taste

Directions

1. Place all the ingredients in a mixing bowl and combine well, then allow them to sit for 10 minutes
2. Heat a medium sized, heavy bottomed, fry pan on a medium heat with the coconut oil
3. Using a tablespoon, scoop up the mixture from the bowl and place it into the hot oil cooking about 5 to 6 at a time. Slightly flatten each fritter and cook them for 3 to 4 minutes each side or until they are golden brown.
4. They can be served hot, warm or at room temperature

Kale and Tofu Basket

Makes 2 servings

This nutritious mixture of vegetables gives you a high powered protein and vitamin breakfast to last the whole morning so you don't feel the need to snack until lunch time.

Ingredients

- 6 to 8 large Kale leaves with the hard ribs removed and torn into bite sized pieces
- 12 ounces of extra firm Tofu, (marinated or plain), cut into ¾ inch cubes
- ½ a cup of Pickled Cabbage or Sauerkraut
- 2 tbsp of Nutritional Yeast
- 1 to 2 tbsp of Coconut Oil
- Some coarse Sea Salt

Optional toppings

- Sun-dried Tomatoes, Mushrooms, Aubergines, Mushrooms or Fruit of your choice
- Radishes thinly sliced
- Kale Pesto

- Nut Crème or Butter
- A poached Organic Egg
- Sliced Avocado
- Tomato, Chili, or Salsa

Directions

1. Place a little coconut oil in a large, heavy bottomed pan and heat it to a medium temperature
2. Sprinkle the tofu with the coarse salt and sauté it in the hot oil until golden brown, about 7 minutes, keep stirring and brown on all sides
3. Once browned, sprinkle the yeast over the tofu and stir it so it is evenly coated
4. Then lower the heat and add the kale with about 2 tbsp of water so the kale steams and wilts down
5. Place it all in a serving bowl and add the pickled cabbage and the toppings you desire

Kale Pesto Pizza

Makes two 9 inch pizzas or one, 12 inches

This pizza recipe uses the same pesto recipe described earlier and with additional kale and sun-dried tomatoes for the topping

Ingredients

- 1 pound of pizza dough, store bought or make your own by thoroughly mixing together a cup of flour, a tbsp. of yeast, a tsp. of sugar, a dash of salt and then add ½ a cup of lukewarm water and mix until smooth. Cover and set aside to rise for 30 minutes then roll out to the desired shape
- 2 cups of grated Mozzarella Cheese
- 2 tbsp of grated Parmesan (or any other tasty cheese)
- 1 cup of packed Kale with stem removed and torn into bite sized pieces
- 1 tsp of Olive Oil
- ¼ of a cup of thinly sliced Sun-dried Tomatoes
- ¼ of a tsp of fine Sea Salt

- Sea Salt and freshly Cracked Black Pepper to taste

Directions

1. Preheat your oven to 500F
2. Place the prepared kale in a small bowl and add the oil and salt. Then massage the oil evenly over all parts of the kale.
3. Roll out the pizza dough to your desired size and place in pizza pans or if you are using a pizza stone in oven, make the pizza on parchment paper to make lifting and transferring onto the hot stone in the oven easier
4. Top your pizza(s) with a nice even layer of pesto and sprinkle some Mozzarella on top, then add the kale and sun-dried tomatoes evenly over the pizza. Add a little more Mozzarella and Parmesan
5. Bake until the cheese on top is bubbling and the crust I golden brown
6. Slice and serve

Spicy Kale and Coconut Stir-fry

Makes enough for 2 servings

This flavorful, easy to prepare and cook stir-fry is reminiscent of dining in Thailand, it brings back fond memories of sunsets and clear water beaches.

Ingredients

- 1 large bunch of Kale with the thick ribs removed
- ¾ of a cup of diagonally sliced spring onions
- 1 small Carrot, sliced thinly
- 2 stalks of Celery
- 1 small Green pepper, sliced thinly
- 1 small Red or Yellow pepper, sliced thinly
- 4 Brussel Sprouts, sliced thinly
- 3 cloves of Garlic, minced
- 2 small fresh Limes
- A 1/4 inch piece of Ginger, finely sliced
- 2 Eggs, lightly beaten with a pinch of Sea Salt

- ¾ cup of large Coconut Flakes (do not use shredded)
- 2 cups of cooked Brown Rice
- 2 tsp of Chili Sauce
- 2 tsp of Tamari Sauce
- 1 tbsp of Oyster Sauce
- Coconut Oil or Ghee for cooking
- 1 handful of fresh herbs of your choice for a garnish

Directions

1. Heat your 12 inch wok or large fry pan to a medium heat and place in it 1 tsp. of oil. Cook the eggs until just set and then place them in a large bowl
2. Add about a tbsp. of oil in the wok and add the ginger first. Allow this to cook while stirring for about a minute, then add the garlic, carrots, celery, brussel sprouts and capsicum. Cook until just tender. Then place in the bowl on top of the eggs

3. Place 2 tsp. of oil in the wok and cook the coconut flakes until they are just golden brown, then add the rice stirring and cooking until heated through.
4. Once heated through, add the contents of the bowl back into the wok and add the chili, tamari and oyster sauces as well as the juice of 1 lime
5. Stir the mixture and serve in bowls with lime wedges and herbs as a garnish

Kale and Seafood Linguine

Makes enough for 3 to 4 large servings

The slightly bitter taste of the kale makes an enjoyable contrast to the sweetness of scallops and prawns and the spiciness of the Nduja (hot spicy salami). For those who are not partial to spicy foods, the nduja can be replaced with ham or cooked chicken.

Ingredients

- 3 oz. of Kale with the hard ribs removed
- ½ lb. of shelled Scallops with their roe
- ½ lb. of live Clams in the shell
- ½ lb. of live Mussels in the shell
- ½ lb. of shelled Tiger Prawns
- 8 oz. of Linguine or Fettucine
- 2 oz. of Nduja (soft hot spicy Salami)
- 2 cloves of Garlic, finely chopped
- 2 oz. of Dry White Wine (A nice drinking wine)
- 2 oz. of heavy Cream
- 2 tbsp of Olive Oil
- 1 small lemon, zested then cut into serving wedges

- Fresh Shaved Parmesan Cheese
- Freshly cracked Black Pepper

Directions

1. Cook the linguine until just under done in a large saucepan of salted water
2. Heat the olive oil in a large wok on a medium temperature and add the nduja. Break it up into the oil using a spoon, then add the garlic and cook until it becomes fragrant - about 1 minute
3. Turn up the heat and add all the seafood stirring to combine and after 2 minutes, add the kale, wine and cream
4. Place a lid on top and cook for about 3 minutes, then give a good stir. Remove any clams or mussels that did not open.
5. Drain the linguine and pour the sauce over it. Toss gently to combine. Stir in the lemon zest and garnish with the shaved parmesan, black pepper and lemon wedges

Cheesy Kale Casserole

Makes enough for 4 servings

This cheesy kale casserole is ideal for people who have not tried to eat kale before, it is a delicious and filling casserole that keeps well and can be frozen

Ingredients

- 10 ounces of fresh Kale with the stalks and ribs removed
- 1 pound of lean ground beef
- 2 cups of Marinara Sauce
- 4 ounces of Shredded Mozzarella Cheese
- 1 tsp of Garlic powder
- 1 tsp of Onion Powder
- 1 tsp of Oregano Leaves
- 1 tsp of Sea Salt
- ½ of a tsp of Ground Black Pepper
- 2 tbsp of Coconut or Olive Oil

Directions

1. Place the oil in a large, heavy bottomed pan on a medium to high heat
2. Add the beef when the oil is hot and break it up with a spoon so it does not clump together.

3. Continue cooking and stirring until all the beef is cooked, about 5 to 7 minutes
4. Then stir in the Garlic powder, onion powder, oregano, salt and pepper.
5. Stir the kale into the beef mixture and cook until it starts to wilt
6. Add the marinara sauce and continue cooking and stirring until it is all heated through
7. Add half of the mozzarella cheese and stir to combine
8. Sprinkle the rest of the cheese on top and place the casserole under an overhead grill (broiler) so the cheese melts
9. Allow the casserole to rest for 5 minutes, then serve

Marinated Beef and Kale Stew

Makes enough to serve 4 to 6 people

The stew has a deep, rich flavor from being marinated in red wine. The kale provides added vitamins as well as a nice contrasting texture. By stirring in some fresh squeezed lemon juice just before serving you will brighten all the flavors

Ingredients

- 2 large bunches of Kale, storks and ribs removed
- 2 pounds of Beef such as Chuck or Round Roast
- 2 Carrots, Large cubed
- 1 Large Onion, diced
- 2 cloves of minced Garlic
- 1 bottle of nice Dry Red Wine
- 10 whole Black Peppercorns
- 1 Bouquet garni made of 1 sprig of Parsley, 1 sprig of Rosemary and a Bay Leaf
- 2 cups of Stock of your choice
- Coconut Oil for cooking
- Sea Salt to taste

Direction

1. Place the beef, carrot, onion, garlic, wine, peppercorns and bouquet garni in a large food safe container and marinate everything in the refrigerator for a minimum of 4 hours up to a maximum of 24 hours
2. Before you start cooking, first drain the stew by passing it through a colander into another container so you can set aside and retain the liquid to use later in the recipe
3. Place the beef cubes on paper towels and pat them dry, once dried season them with sea salt and pepper
4. Place a large, heavy bottomed stock pot on a medium heat and add 2 tablespoons of coconut oil. When the oil is hot, carefully place each piece of beef in the oil, leaving enough spaces between them so they will fry not boil in their own juices. This is an important step as if allowed to boil the meat will become tough and will not be as

flavorful. You may need to do them in batches. Try to give each piece a nice deep brown crust all sides.

5. Place the meat once browned on a dish to rest while you cook the next batch. Once all the beef is browned and out of the stockpot, lower the heat and place all the vegetables in it
6. Cook the vegetables for about 5 minutes, stirring constantly to stop them burning and when they soften, add the browned beef, stock and marinade.
7. Simmer the stew stirring frequently and to deglaze the bottom of the pot
8. Simmer the stew for 60 to 90 minutes
9. About 15 minutes before the stew is finished cooking, prepare your kale, by tearing it into bite sized pieces, then add it to the stew.
10. Keep simmering the stew for about 10 minutes, the kale should be bright green and tender. Check the seasoning by tasting and adjust if necessary, then add

a little lemon juice just before serving

and enjoy

Kale, Chicken, Mushrooms and Noodles

Makes enough for 4 servings

This quick to make chicken noodle dish has crunchy beans, delicious mushrooms and tasty kale ideal for a quick weekend dinner. When cooking stir-fry, you need to work quickly so that nothing gets overcooked or cools down too much

Ingredients

- 3 oz. of Kale Leaves with the ribs removed
- 1 ½ lbs. of Chicken Breasts sliced into strips
- 1 cup of Green Beans, stringed and topped
- 1 ½ cups of Mushrooms, sliced
- 8 oz. of Udon Noodles
- 2 tsp of crushed Garlic
- 2 tsp of Chia seeds
- ½ a tsp of finely mince Ginger

Directions

1. Place a large wok over a high heat with a very small amount of oil and add your almonds tossing them rapidly or stirring constantly so they do not burn. They will become fragrant, very quickly about 30 seconds and then they should be removed from the heat and set to the side
2. In the same large wok, add a little more oil and cook your chicken strips so they are rare, not overdone. Once cooked, set them also to the side
3. Then once again in the same wok, cook your mushrooms, as soon as they start to soften, add the garlic and cook to al dente. Then remove from the heat and set it aside
4. Prepare your noodles in the manner suggested on the packet
5. While the noodles are being cooked or softening, Cook your beans in the wok. Use a little oil and toss them quickly, so they are bright colored and still crunchy

6. Add the chopped kale and chia seeds and stir them through.
7. Add back the chicken and mushrooms
8. Drain the noodles and carefully stir them through your chicken and vegetables
9. Serve the noodles on plates and sprinkle the almonds over the top or place in a serving bowl and add the almonds before serving

Kale Lasagna

Kale is terrific for adding substance and heartiness to this lasagna, giving it nutritional value and texture allowing for a new taste sensation.

Ingredients

- 1 large bunch of Kale, stalks and ribs removed, sliced in ribbons
- One 28 ounce can of whole Plum Tomatoes
- 1 cup of Roasted Red Peppers, diced
- 1 ½ cups of grated Mozzarella Cheese
- 15 ounces of Ricotta Cheese
- 2 large Egg Whites
- ¾ cup of sliced Mushrooms
- 2 cloves of Garlic, thinly sliced
- 9 sheets of no-boil lasagna noodles
- ½ a tsp of dried Oregano
- ¼ of a tsp of crushed Red Pepper Flakes
- ¼ of a tsp of Sugar
- 2 tbsp of coarsely chopped fresh Parsley
- 1 tbsp of Olive Oil

- Sea Salt and freshly cracked Black Pepper as needed

Directions

1. Place the tomatoes, peppers, oregano, ¼of a tsp of salt, ¼ tsp of black pepper and the sugar into your blender or food processor and blender until the mixture is smooth, then set it aside
2. Mix together 1 cup of mozzarella cheese with the egg whites and the ricotta cheese and set these aside
3. Place the oil in a large pan or wok set on a medium to high heat.
4. Add the mushrooms and sauté until they release their juices and become tender
5. Stir in the sliced kale and as it wilts, add the garlic, pepper flakes and ¼ of a tsp of salt
6. Continue sautéing until the kale is totally wilted and bright green in color about 5 minutes
7. Preheat your oven to 375F

To assemble the lasagna

1. Lightly oil a 9 x 13 inch baking dish and spread ¾ of a cup of the tomato sauce, then place 3 of the lasagna sheets on top
2. Spread a layer of ½ of the ricotta and half the kale and mushroom mixture
3. Then another layer of lasagna sheet followed by another layer of tomato sauce, followed with lasagna and topped with the remaining ricotta and kale and mushrooms
4. Cover the lasagna with a lid or a sheet of foil and bake for about 45 minutes or until the sauce is bubbling around the sides and the noodles are tender
5. Remove the top or the foil and sprinkle with the remaining mozzarella cheese and bake under the grill to brown for about 5 minutes.
6. Allow it to stand for about 10 minutes, then garnish with the chopped parsley and serve

Kale and Portobello Mushrooms

Makes a vegetable serving for 4 people

Kale and Portobello Mushrooms make a great side dish to compliment any meal.

Ingredients

- 1 & ¼ pounds of Kale with the stems and ribs removed
- 4 Portobello Mushrooms, sliced
- ½ a cup of nice drinking, Dry Red Wine
- ¼ of a tsp of freshly grated Nutmeg
- 3 tbsp of Extra Virgin Olive Oil
- Sea Salt and freshly cracked Black Pepper as needed

Directions

1. Place a large, heavy bottomed frying pan or saucepan over a medium heat and add the olive oil
2. Add the mushrooms when the oil has become hot and sautee them until they are dark and tender
3. Add the kale and using tongs keep turning it until it wilts.

4. Season with salt and pepper
5. Add the red wine and use it to deglaze the bottom
6. Reduce the heat and simmer until the kale is tender and taste. Adjust the seasoning if necessary, then serve

Kale and Cannellini Bean Stew

Makes enough for 8 servings

Made using a Parmesan, garlic broth, this kale and Cannellini bean (or any other beans you like) is a medium to spicy vegetarian dish brings out the qualities of both **Ingredients**

For the Parmesan Garlic Broth

- 2 quarts of Vegetable Stock or Water
- 1 cup of Dry White Wine
- 1 pound of Parmesan Rinds
- 1 large Onion, finely diced
- 2 bulbs of Garlic with the cloves crushed
- A Bouquet garni made using 4 fresh Thyme sprigs, 4 fresh Sage Sprigs, 3 fresh or dried Bay Leaves and A dozen fresh Parsley sprigs
- 1 tsp of whole Black Peppercorns
- 1 tsp of allspice
- 6 whole Cloves
- ¼ of a tsp of Celery Seeds
- ¼ of a tsp of Coriander Seeds
- 1 tsp of Sea Salt
- 2 tbsp of Coconut Oil

For the Stew

- A large bunch of Kale with the hard stalks and ribs removed
- 1 cup of diced Carrots
- 1 cup of sliced Celery Stalks
- 2.5 cups of diced Onion
- 3 large cloves of Garlic, thinly sliced
- A 15 oz. can of diced Tomatoes
- 4 x 15 oz. cans of Cannellini Beans, drained
- ¼ of a cup of Red Wine Vinegar
- 8 thick slices of Bread
- Shaved Parmesan for the bread
- Red Pepper Flakes for a garnish

To make the broth

1. Place the oil in a large, heavy bottomed saucepan and sauté the onion, garlic and salt until tender and just golden brown.
2. Add the stock wine, Bouquet garni spices and Parmesan Rinds and bring to the boil. Then reduce the heat until you have a slow simmer. Simmer until the

liquid is reduced by about half, approximately 2 hours

3. Strain the broth through a fine sieve and press to remove all the liquid. There should be about 4 cups and a little water if needed

To make the stew

1. Place the oil in a large, heavy bottomed saucepan and when hot, add the onions, carrots, celery, garlic as well as a large pinch each of salt and cracked black pepper. Sauté for about 10 minutes and then add the broth, tomatoes, beans and a little more salt.
2. Simmer the stew for about 15 minutes and taste it, then adjust the seasoning if necessary
3. Brush one side of the bread with oil and toast it, then brush the other side and put the shaved Parmesan on top before toasting.

Place the toasted Parmesan bread in each of your serving bowls and ladle the stew on top, garnish with the red pepper flakes and serve

Kale and Pork Casserole

Makes a serving for 4 people

Kale and pork casserole is a great comfort food, it satisfies our sweet, fatty and sour taste buds as well as making a filling meal.

Ingredients

- 4 cups of Kale with the stalks and ribs removed
- 1 pound of Pork Loin, trimmed and cubed
- 2 cups of Chicken or Vegetable Stock
- 3 cups of Potatoes, cubed
- 1 cup of Onion, Diced
- 1 cup of Carrots, julienned
- 3 cloves of Garlic, minced
- 1 tbsp of Paprika
- 2 tsp of Oregano
- 1 tsp of freshly made Mustard
- ½ a tsp of Chili Powder
- ¼ of a tsp of Black Pepper
- 1/8 of a tsp of Cayenne Pepper
- Coconut Oil or Ghee for cooking

Directions

1. Combine all the spices together and rub them into the pork so they completely cover the pieces
2. Place a heavy, bottomed skillet on a high heat and add the oil
3. When the oil is hot, add the pork a piece at a time and sear it on all sides (do not add too much or the juices will come out and the pork will boil becoming tough)
4. Cook the pork for about 5 minutes, then add the onions, carrot and Garlic and simmer for about 10 minutes
5. Add the potatoes and the broth
6. Simmer for about 25 to 30 minutes covered
7. Add the kale and simmer about another 10 minutes

Taste and adjust the seasoning if required and when the potatoes are tender serve

Savory Kale Chips

Makes a snack for 3 to 4 people

Kale chips are a very popular snack which can make a healthy alternative to conventional processed potato chips.

Ingredients

- A good sized bunch of Fresh Kale Leaves
- 1 tbsp of Coconut or good quality Olive Oil

For the spice

- 1.5 tbsp of Nutritional Yeast
- 1 tsp of Garlic Powder
- ¾ of a tsp of Red Chili Powder
- ½ a tsp of Onion Powder
- ½ a tsp of Smoked Paprika
- ¼ of a tsp of Black Cumin Powder
- ¼ of a tsp of Ground Celery Seeds
- ¼ of a tsp of fine Sea Salt
- 1/8 of a tsp of Cayenne Pepper

Directions

1. Preheat your oven to 300F
2. Line a large baking tray or 2 with parchment paper
3. Take the hard stem from the kale leaves and tear the leaves into bite sized pieces
4. Thoroughly wash the leaves and then dry them completely. This can be done with paper towels or a lettuce spinner, but the leaves must be dry - otherwise they will steam and become soggy
5. Place the dried leaves in a large bowl and add the oil, massaging into into all parts of the leaves
6. Mix all the spice ingredients together and sprinkle over the leaves then toss to combine and cover the leaves
7. Spread the leaves out in one layer on the parchment paper. Ensure the leaves are not overcrowded, so they will bake rather than steam
8. Bake the kale for about 10 minutes, then turn the leaves and bake for about another 10 to 15 minutes or until they

become firm. Note they will have shrunk and when removed from the oven will continue to firm up on the trays if left for about 3 minutes.

9. Cook them as required as they need to be consumed straight away rather than stored, because they will lose their crispness quickly.

Do not add any liquids before cooking as this will cause them to steam rather than bake and result in soggy limp leaves. If you wish to add a liquid seasoning, do so after they are cooked or use as a dipping sauce.

Kale Ice Cream

Makes about 1 and a half Quarts

This very tasty vegetable ice cream is made using sweet potatoes, kale, cream cheese and spices.

Ingredients

- 5 cups of fresh Kale that has had the stalks and hard ribs removed, the is blanches in boiling water before being chilled
- 2 medium sized Sweet Potatoes, peeled and chopped in small cubes
- ¾ of a cup of Raw Sugar
- 2 cups of Half and Half or Cream
- 8 ounces of softened Cream Cheese
- 2 tbsp of Unsweetened Butter
- 2 tsp of Vanilla Essence
- ¼ of a tsp of Cinnamon
- ¼ of a tsp of Nutmeg
- 1/8 of a tsp of Sea Salt

Directions

1. Heat a large, heavy bottomed saucepan on a medium heat and melt the butter until it is totally melted
2. Add the sweet potatoes and ¼ of a tsp of salt and simmer them on a low heat covered for about 10 minutes stirring occasionally.
3. Then turn up the heat and cook them until they become very soft, they will need constant stirring to avoid burning. Continue cooking until they start to brown, then turn off the heat and allow them to cool slightly
4. Placed the cooled sweet potato in a food processor or blender and puree them with ¼ of a cup of half and half or cream. Then place them in a separate bowl
5. Place the blanched kale in your blender with the sugar, cream cheese and add the rest of the half and half as well as the spices. Blend this on high until well combined

6. Then blend the sweet potatoes, the kale and cream cheese mixture together
7. Season to taste with salt
8. Pass the mixture through a colander or fine sieve, then place in a food safe air tight container and place it in the freezer until it becomes very cold. Approximately 3 hours
9. If you have an ice cream maker, then churn it in that following the manufactures instructions
10. If you do not have an ice cream maker the alternative is to leave it in the freezer until it starts to freeze, then re-blend it to break up the ice crystals. It will have to be re-frozen and then blended several times.
11. Before serving, remove it from your freezer 15 minutes before serving and it will be easier use

Kale Cake with a Sweet Potato Filling

Makes 6 to 8 slices

This vegan recipe contains a small amount of sugar and is a great treat to end a meal or have as a healthy snack anytime.

Ingredients

Cake Ingredients

- 2 cups of Kale that has been blanched, cooled and finely chopped
- 1 cup of Walnuts, chopped up
- 2 1/3 cups of All-Purpose Flour
- 1 cup of Raw Sugar
- 1 cup of Coconut Oil
- ¾ of a cup of Water
- 6 tbsp of Flax Seed Meal
- 1 tbsp of Vanilla Essence
- 1 ½ tsp of Baking Soda
- 1 tsp of Baking Powder
- 1 tsp of Cinnamon
- ½ a tsp of Nutmeg
- ½ a tsp of fine Sea Salt

For the cake filling

- 2 Sweet Potatoes, peeled, diced and boiled, then blended until they are smooth
- 2 cups of Almond Milk
- 1/3 of a cup of Sugar
- 2 tbsp of Arrowroot
- 1 tbsp of Vegan Margarine
- 2 tsp of Vanilla Extract
- ¼ of a tsp of fine Sea Salt
- A pinch of Nutmeg

Icing Ingredients

- Two x 8 ounce containers of Cream Cheese
- ½ a cup of Vegan Margarine
- ¾ to 1 ½ cups of powdered Raw Sugar
- 1 tsp of Vanilla Essence

Filling Directions

1. Place the arrowroot and sugar in a heavy bottomed saucepan and whisk them together

2. Add the sweet potato and almond milk, then whisk this mixture until there are no lumps
3. Place the saucepan over a medium heat and continuously whisk it until the custard thickens to the point where, if you coat the back of a wooden spoon with the custard. Then run your finger through it the tail will not close up
4. When the custard is thick enough, remove it from the heat
5. Whisk in the vegan margarine, vanilla and the nutmeg
6. Place the custard in a new bowl with a plastic sheet placed right on the surface to prevent a skin forming there

Directions for the Cake

1. Preheat your oven to 350F
2. Line two 8 inch by 8 inch cake pans with parchment paper
3. Sift together the flour and salt to fully combine and aerate them
4. Whisk the flax seed meal and the water together in a large mixing bowl

5. Beat the sugar and oil into the flax seed mixture
6. Add the vanilla and blanched kale together and mix these until they are fully combined
7. Add the flour and salt mixture and stir this until it is completely moistened, then fold in the walnuts
8. Pour the batter equally into the two parchment paper lined cake pans
9. Bake them in the preheated oven for about 18 minutes or until, when you insert a toothpick into the center of the cake, it comes out clean

Icing Directions

1. Beat the cream cheese and vegan butter together
2. Add the powdered sugar and vanilla essence and whip this mixture just until it is smooth, but avoid over beating it
3. When the cakes have cooled, they will probably need to be loosened from the pans with a knife

4. Carefully lift the cakes from the pans using the parchment and then peel the parchment paper away from the cakes
5. Frost one of the cakes with the sweet potato filling mixture
6. Place the other cake on top of the frosted cake
7. Frost the top and sides of the layered cake with the icing mixture
8. The cake should be placed in the refrigerator to cool before serving chilled

Kale Ice Candy

Makes about a dozen, depending on the size of your molds

This ice candy treat tastes great and is also very good for you. Many people would be surprised that it contains lots of kale. The fruit can be pre frozen if preferred, we often freeze any surplus ripe bananas we have because they make great smoothies or can be used in these ice candies.

Ingredients

- 2 cups of Kale with the stalks and hard ribs removed
- 3 large ripe Bananas
- 16 whole Strawberries or any other sweetish Berry

Directions

1. Clean the strawberries by rinsing with a solution made of 2 tsp. of baking soda to a pint of water, this will remove any dirt or dust and also take away any wax or chemicals on the delicate fruit's surface
2. The kale should also be rinsed, you can use the same solution then fresh water
3. Peel the banana

4. Place all the ingredients in your food processor or blender and puree them until smooth. If you like a less smooth texture, just pulse them until you get the consistency and texture you desire
5. Once blended place or pour the mixture into freezer pop molds and freeze, then enjoy

Kale Chocolate Cake

Makes about 8 to 12 slices

This chocolate cake is very healthy so you can indulge without the need of feeling guilty or worry you are not being health conscious.

Ingredients for the Cake

- 3 cups of Kale with their stems and hard ribs removed, then finely chopped
- 2 cups of All-purpose Flour
- 4 ounces of Semi Sweet Chocolate
- ¼ of a cup of Cocoa Powder
- ¾ of a cup of Sour Cream
- 1 cup of Unsalted Butter at room temperature
- 1 ¾ cups of Raw Sugar
- 4 large Eggs
- 1 tsp of Vanilla Extract
- 1 ½ tsp of Baking Powder
- ¾ of a tsp of Baking Soda
- 1 tsp of fine Sea Salt

Ingredients for the Frosting

- 2 sticks of Unsalted Butter at room temperature

- 3 ½ cups of Sugar that has been sifted
- ½ a cup of Cocoa Powder that has been sifted
- ½ a tsp of fine Sea Salt
- 2 tsp of Vanilla Extract
- 4 tbsp of Full Cream

Directions

1. Lightly grease two 8 inch by 8 inch cake pans with butter, then dust them with cocoa powder
2. Place a saucepan with a little water on the heat to boil then place the chocolate in a bowl in the boiling water to melt. When the chocolate has melted, blanch the kale for 2 minutes
3. Then place the kale in your food processor or blender and puree until it's smooth (add a little water if needed). Then remove any fibers by straining the kale

4. Add ¾ of a cup of cooked kale to the chocolate and then add the cocoa powder
5. Add the sour cream and whisk it all together to combine
6. Beat together the sugar and butter until fluffy and light
7. Add in the eggs, one at a time, beating to combine before adding the next
8. In a separate medium bowl, whisk together the flour, salt, soda and baking powder
9. Mix together the cakes by adding the butter mixture and flour mixtures to the kale bowl to totally combine the batter
10. Preheat your oven to 350F
11. Pour the batter equally into the two parchment lined cake pans
12. Bake for 30 to 35 minutes, they are ready when you insert a toothpick into the center of the cake, it comes out clean
13. When cooked, take the cakes from the oven and allow them to sit for 10

minutes before removing and placing
them on wire racks to cool

To make the Frosting

1. Sift the sugar and cocoa together
2. Cream the butter and add the sugar, cocoa, salt and vanilla extract together
3. The frosting will for after you beat this mixture for about 3 minutes

When the cake is completely cooled, frost the top of one cake, then place it on top of the other and frost the top and sides

Greek Kale and Avocado Salad

Makes 8 servings

This hearty and colorful salad is an ideal addition to compliment any dish or even a complete meal on its own, especially if you add some cooked chicken or seafood.

Ingredients

- 4 cups of fresh Kale leaves with their stems removed then torn into bite sized pieces
- 1 large Avocado, peeled, stoned and sliced
- 1 medium Cucumber, diced
- 1 cup of ripe Cherry Tomatoes, sliced in half
- 1 medium Red Pepper, deseeded and sliced thinly
- 1 medium Green Pepper, deseeded and sliced thinly
- 1 medium Red Onion, Sliced thinly
- 1 cup of Artichoke Hearts, halved
- ¼ of a cup of Green Olives
- ¼ of a cup of Black Olives

- ½ a cup of Fresh chopped Basil or 2 tsp of dried
- ½ a cup of fresh Feta Cheese, diced or crumbled

The Dressing

1. ¼ of a cup of Olive Oil or 50/50 Olive and Avocado Oils
2. The juice of one Lemon or lemon and Lime
3. 1 of a tsp of Dried Oregano
4. ½ of a tsp of Dried Basil
5. ¼ of a tsp of Dried Thyme
6. ½ of a tsp of Garlic Powder
7. ¼ of a tsp of Freshly Cracked Black Pepper
8. ¼ of a tsp of Sea Salt

Directions

Place all the dressing ingredients in a bowl and whisk them together and allow them to infuse while making the salad

Combine all the salad ingredients in a large bowl and toss them with the dressing

Kale, Apple, Almond and Cheddar Salad with Fresh Parsley

Makes a salad for 2 people

A quick and refreshing, tasty salad that's perfect for a slimming lunch

Ingredients

- 4 cups of Curly Kale, finely sliced
- 2 tbsp of coarsely chopped roasted Nuts of your choice
- 1 whole Green Apple, diced
- 1.5 ounces of Extra Tasty Cheddar, cut into ¼ inch cubes
- 1 tbsp of Fresh Lemon Juice
- 1 tbsp of Fresh Lime Juice
- 1 clove of minced Garlic
- 2 tbsp of freshly shaved Parmesan Cheese
- 5 tbsp of Extra Virgin Olive Oil
- 3 tbsp of fresh, finely chopped Parsley
- Sea Salt and freshly cracked Black Pepper to taste

Directions

1. Combine together the kale, apple, almonds and cheddar in a large serving bowl
2. Whisk the lemon, lime, olive oil, garlic and salt together and toss it into the salad turning to evenly coat everything.
3. Sprinkle the parmesan and parsley over the top and serve

Kale and Toasted Walnut Pesto

Makes about 4 servings

This tasty pesto can be used as a dip, a spread or added to your favorite pasta to make wholesome meal.

Ingredients

- 2 cups of fresh packed Kale with the stems removed
- 1 cup of fresh Basil Leaves
- ½ a cup of freshly shaved or grated Parmesan Cheese
- 1/3 of a cup of freshly toasted Walnuts
- 4 to 6 cloves of fresh chopped Garlic
- ¼ of a cup of Extra Virgin Olive Oil
- 1 tsp of fine Sea Salt

Directions

1. Place the kale leaves, basil and salt in your blender or food processor and pulse until they are finely shredded.
2. With the motor running on medium, slowly pour the olive oil until combined

3. Scrape the sides of the processor and add the garlic and walnuts and pulse again until combined.

If you are using straight away add the Parmesan now or wait until just before using for the best results

Crisp Kale Bars

Makes 10 medium sized bars

These crispy kale bars are great for school snacks or for snacks when in the great outdoors.

Ingredients

- A large bunch of fresh Kale
- 1 tbsp of Coconut Oil
- 1 cup of Quick Cooking Oats
- 1/3 of a cup of Sunflower or Pumpkin Seeds
- 2 tbsp of Sunflower Seeds
- 1 cup puffed Whole Grain Cereal such as Quinoa or Rice
- 1/3 of a cup of dried Berries such as Cherries, Cranberries etc.
- 1/3 of a cup of Almond or Cashew Butter
- ¼ of a cup of Natural Organic Cane Sugar
- ¼ of a cup of Raw Honey, Maple Syrup of Molasses
- ¼ of a tsp of fine Sea Salt
- ¼ of a tsp of Vanilla or Almond Extract

Direction

1. Preheat your oven to 300F
2. Line an 8 inch square pan with parchment paper and lightly brush it with coconut oil to stop the kale sticking
3. Prepare the kale by removing the hard stems and then washing it well in water.
4. Completely dry the kale with paper towels or in a lettuce spinner
5. Then place them in a bowl with the oil and massage the oil over all parts of the leaves to coat
6. Bake the kale for about 15 minutes or until the leaves have shrunk and become firm. Do not allow them to become brown. Once cooked, remove on the parchment and cool
7. Bake the oats and seeds in the oven until they are fragrant and golden
8. Transfer the oats and seeds to a mixing bowl and combine with the berries and cereal
9. Crumble the cooled kale leaves into the mixture and stir to combine

10. Place the nut butter, sugar, honey and salt in a heavy bottomed saucepan and heat them on a low to medium heat until the sugar is dissolved and the mixture is smooth. Then remove it from the heat and stir in the extract
11. While still hot, pour the nut butter and sugar mixture over the oats and stir to combine, then pour the whole mixture into your prepared dish as in instruction 1
12. Oil a sheet of plastic film and place in on top of the mixture in your pan and use this to spread and compress the mixture evenly
13. When the mixture is flat and even place it in the refrigerator to cool and set for several hours
14. Remove the mixture from the pan using the parchment paper and cut it on a cutting board into 10 even sized bars. Then wrap them individually in plastic before storing in your refrigerator for up to a week or 3 months in the freezer

Kale, Blackberry and Chocolate Smoothie

Makes 4 servings

This mouth-watering smoothie combines kale and the high protein of chocolate whey powder with the richness of almond butter and the goodness of blackberries, coconut and bananas.

Ingredients

- 6 to 7 large Kale Leaves, with their hard stork removed then sliced to fit your blender
- 2 medium peeled and sliced frozen Bananas
- 3 tbsp of Chocolate Protein Powder
- 2 cups of Coconut Milk
- ½ a cup of unsweetened shredded Coconut
- 1 tbsp of Almond Butter
- ½ a cup of frozen Blackberries (or berries of your choice)
- ½ a cup of fresh water to use as needed

Directions

Place all of the ingredients in your blender or food processor and blend them on high until smooth.

Kale, High Calcium Smoothie

Makes 2 servings

This is super high calcium and antioxidant smoothie is great for everyone to round off the diet and detox.

Ingredients

- 1 cup of packed Baby Kale
- 1/3 of a cup of Parsley
- 6 medium Carrots
- 4 stalks of Celery with leaves
- 1 whole Cucumber
- 1 whole Green Apple Seeds and skin included
- ½ inch piece of Green Ginger

Directions

Place all of the ingredients in your blender or food processor and blend them on high until smooth.

Tips on using Kale in smoothies

Kale is easy to freeze to maintain in optimum condition for using in your smoothies at any time. Cut away the hard rib from the leaves and give it a good rinse. Then freeze it. This helps to make it taste less bitter and also cool down your smoothie.

Or if preferred it can be blanched until soft before freezing. This will help to break down its cellular structure, increasing its digestibility and helping you to easily absorb its many nutrients.

Chapter 11:
Anti-cancer Chia Seed Recipes

Coconut Chia Pudding

Serves: 2

Ingredients:

- ½ cup coconut milk
- ½ cup raspberries, fresh or frozen + extra to garnish
- ½ teaspoon vanilla powder or 1 teaspoon vanilla extract
- ¼ cup water
- ¼ cup chia seeds
- Sweetener of your choice to taste (optional)

Directions:

1. Add water, coconut milk and raspberries into a blender and blend until smooth.
2. Add rest of the ingredients and stir.
3. Cover and chill for a few hours.
4. Serve in glasses, topped with raspberries.

Chia and Flaxseed Microwave Oatmeal

Serves: 2

Ingredients:

- 3 tablespoons rolled oats
- 1 teaspoon chia seeds
- ½ tablespoon nut butter
- Honey to taste
- ¼ cup milk of your choice
- ½ tablespoon flaxseed meal
- Ground cinnamon to taste
- Toppings of your choice like seeds, nuts, dried fruits or fresh fruits

Directions:

1. Add milk, oats and chia seeds into a microwave safe bowl. Microwave on High for about 3 minutes.
2. Remove from the microwave and stir in rest of the ingredients.
3. Top with the toppings of your choice and serve.Coconut Chia Protein Pancakes

Serves: 4

Ingredients:

- ½ cup gluten free all-purpose flour
- 6 tablespoons vanilla whey protein powder
- A large pinch sea salt

- 2 tablespoons coconut flakes
- ½ cup almond milk
- 4 tablespoons coconut flour
- 1 teaspoon baking powder
- 2 tablespoons chia seeds
- 2 eggs
- Coconut oil to fry

Directions:

1. Add flour, protein powder, salt, coconut flour, coconut flakes and chia seeds into a bowl. Mix well.
2. Add eggs and almond milk and whisk until well combined.
3. Place a nonstick pan over medium heat. Add a about a teaspoon of oil. When the oil melts, pour 2-3 tablespoons of batter. In a while bubbles will appear on the top. Cook until the bottom is brown. Turn over and cook the other side too
4. Repeat with the remaining batter.
5. Serve with a topping of your choice like maple syrup, honey, berries etc.

Coconut Crunch French toast with Guava Syrup

Serves: 4

Ingredients:

For guava syrup:

- 2 cups guava puree
- 2 tablespoons palm sugar
- 2 cups water
- 2 tablespoons chia seeds

For French toast:

- 4 large eggs
- ½ cup heavy cream
- 1 tablespoon vanilla extract
- ¼ teaspoon ground nutmeg
- 2 cups coconut crunch pieces or coconut flakes
- Butter, as required
- Oil, as required
- 2 cups milk
- 4 tablespoons light brown sugar
- 1 teaspoon ground cinnamon
- 8 slices Hawaiian sweet bread or Brioche or any other sweet bread
- Confectioners' sugar to dust

Directions:

1. To make guava syrup: Add all the ingredients of guava syrup into a saucepan and bring to the boil.
2. Reduce the heat to low and simmer until thick. Turn off the heat. Cover and set aside.
3. For French toast: Add eggs, cream milk and sugar into a bowl and whisk well. Add vanilla and spices and whisk until the sugar is dissolved.
4. Place coconut crunch pieces in a dish.
5. Place a large skillet over medium heat. Add about 2 tablespoons butter and 1-2 tablespoons oil. Let the pan heat.
6. Dip a bread slice in the egg mixture. Shake to drop excess egg. Dredge the slice in coconut crunch. Press lightly and place the bread in the pan. Quickly repeat the process and place 3-4 slices of bread.
7. Cook until the bottom is brown. Turn over and cook the other side too. Remove and place on a serving plate. Sprinkle confectioners' sugar on top. Drizzle warm guava syrup on top and serve.
8. Repeat the above 3 steps with the remaining bread slices.

Spinach Omelet

Serves: 1

Ingredients:

- 2 eggs
- 1 teaspoon chia seeds
- ½ cup tomatoes, chopped
- 1 teaspoon olive oil
- 1 cup baby spinach
- Salt to taste
- Pepper to taste

Directions:

1. Add eggs into a bowl and beat well. Add salt and pepper and beat again.
2. Place a small nonstick pan over medium heat. Add oil. When the oil is heated, add spinach, chia seeds and tomatoes and sauté for a couple of minutes.
3. Pour egg on top and swirl the pan so that the egg spreads.
4. Cook until the eggs are set. Gently slide the omelet onto a plate and serve with toast.

Tomato and Lentil Soup

Serves: 3

Ingredients:

- 1 tablespoon olive oil
- 1 stick celery, sliced
- 2 cloves garlic, finely chopped
- 6 tablespoons red lentils, rinsed
- 3 large ripe tomatoes, chopped
- 1 tablespoon milled chia seeds
- 1 carrot, chopped
- 1 medium onion, chopped
- 2 ½ cups vegetable stock
- 1 can (15 ounces) plum tomatoes
- ½ small bunch fresh basil, chopped
- Salt to taste
- Pepper to taste

Directions:

1. Place a saucepan over medium heat. Add oil. When the oil is heated, add carrots, onion and celery and sauté until onions are translucent.
2. Add garlic and sauté for a few seconds until fragrant.
3. Add stock and bring to the boil. Add lentils and both the tomatoes. Let it boil.
4. Lower heat and cover with a lid. Simmer until lentils are tender.
5. Turn off heat. Add basil and chia seeds. Stir.

6. Blend with an immersion blender until smooth.
7. Add salt and pepper.
8. Ladle into soup bowls and serve.

Creamy Coconut and Carrot Soup

Serves: 2

Ingredients:

- 7 ounces canned coconut milk
- Salt to taste
- 1 teaspoon Thai yellow or red curry paste
- 6 ounces baby carrots, quartered sideways
- 1 tablespoon fresh lime juice
- 6 teaspoons chia seeds
- 1 small yellow onion, chopped
- 1 teaspoon fresh ginger, peeled, grated
- 1 clove garlic, peeled, chopped
- 1 ½ cups vegetable broth or more if required
- ¼ cup fresh cilantro sprigs
- A handful fresh cilantro, chopped

Directions:

1. Place a saucepan over medium high heat. Add 2-3 tablespoons coconut milk.
2. Add onion and salt and cook until soft.
3. Add ginger, garlic and sauté for a minute or so until fragrant.
4. Add rest of the ingredients except chia seeds and stir. Bring to the boil.
5. Lower heat and cover with a lid. Simmer until carrots are tender.
6. Discard cilantro sprigs. Blend the soup with an immersion blender until smooth.

7. Add 5 teaspoons chia seeds and stir.
8. Place the saucepan back on low heat. Simmer until the chia seeds have swelled up.
9. Taste and adjust the seasonings if desired. Add more broth if the soup is very thick.
10. Ladle into soup bowls. Sprinkle cilantro and remaining chia seeds on top and serve.

Creamy Mushroom Soup

Serves: 3

Ingredients:

- ½ pound mushrooms, sliced
- 1 medium onion, chopped
- 1 small tomato, chopped
- 1 stalk celery, chopped
- 1 teaspoon olive oil
- 1 teaspoon sesame oil
- 1 clove garlic, sliced
- Salt to taste
- 1 bay leaf
- Cayenne pepper to taste
- ½ cup chia seeds
- ½ teaspoon tamari or soy sauce or to taste
- ½ cup raw cashews
- 3 cups water

Directions:

1. Add cashew and water into a blender and blend until smooth.
2. Pour into a bowl. Add chia seeds and stir. Set aside for a while.
3. Place a saucepan over medium heat. Add sesame oil. When the oil is heated, add half the mushrooms and sauté for 2-3 minutes. Transfer into the bowl of cashew milk.

4. Place a saucepan over medium heat. Add olive oil. When the oil is heated, add onion, garlic and celery and sauté for a couple of minutes.
5. Add basil and tamari and stir. Add cashew milk. Bring to the boil. Turn off the heat. Cool for awhile and blend with an immersion blender until smooth.
6. Place the saucepan over medium high heat. Add remaining mushrooms, salt and cayenne pepper. Simmer for 10-15 minutes. Add tomatoes during the last 5 minutes of simmering.
7. Ladle into soup bowls and serve.

Peanut Butter Banana Protein Shake

Serves: 2

Ingredients:

- 2 ripe bananas, peeled, sliced
- 1 cup almond milk, unsweetened
- 4 tablespoons peanut butter
- 2 teaspoons chia seeds
- 2 cups ice
- ¼ cup nonfat Greek yogurt
- ½ cup almonds

Directions:

1. Add banana, almond milk, peanut butter, chia seeds, ice, yogurt and almonds into a blender. Blend until smooth.
2. Pour into tall glasses and serve.

Super Foods Smoothie

Serves: 2

Ingredients:

- 1 ½ cups almond milk, unsweetened
- 2/3 cup frozen strawberries
- 1 cup frozen blueberries
- 1 ripe avocado, peeled, pitted, chopped
- 1 cup spinach, torn
- 1 cup berry yogurt
- 2 tablespoons chia seeds
- 2 teaspoons flaxseeds
- 2 scoops greens superfood
- 2 scoops protein powder
- Ice cubes as required

Directions:

1. Add almond milk, strawberries, blueberries, avocado, spinach, berry yogurt, chia seeds, flax seeds, greens superfood, protein powder and ice cubes into a blender.
2. Blend for 30-40 seconds or until smooth. Add more almond milk if you desire a smoothie of thinner consistency.
3. Pour into tall glasses. Garnish with slices of avocado and serve.

Tropical Green Smoothie

Serves: 2

Ingredients:

- 1 banana, sliced, frozen
- 2 cups almond milk or coconut milk
- 2 scoops brown rice protein powder
- 2 teaspoons shredded coconut, unsweetened (optional)
- 1 cup frozen mango
- 3-4 cups baby spinach
- 1 tablespoon chia seeds

Directions:

1. Add banana, milk, protein powder, mango, spinach and chia seeds into a blender and blend until smooth. Add more milk if you desire a smoothie of thinner consistency.
2. Pour into tall glasses. Garnish with shredded coconut and serve.

Blueberry and Agave Smoothie

Serve: 2

Ingredients:

- 4 cups frozen blueberries
- 3 teaspoons chia seeds
- 2 cups orange juice
- 3 teaspoons agave nectar

Directions:

1. Add blueberries, chia seeds, orange juice and agave nectar into a blender.
2. Blend until smooth.
3. Pour into tall glasses and serve with crushed ice.

Snickers Smoothie

Serves: 2

Ingredients:

- 1 cup plain yogurt, unsweetened or plain kefir, unsweetened
- 2 cups almond milk, unsweetened
- Stevia or any other sweetener to taste
- 10 drops English toffee Stevia
- 2 tablespoons cocoa powder, unsweetened
- 2 heaping tablespoons peanut butter or almond butter, unsweetened
- 2 tablespoons vanilla protein powder
- 2 tablespoons chia seeds
- 1 teaspoon vanilla extract
- Ice cubes as required
- Roasted peanuts, crushed to garnish

Directions:

1. Add yogurt, almond milk, Stevia, English toffee Stevia, cocoa powder, peanut butter, vanilla protein powder, chia seeds, vanilla extract and ice cubes into a blender.
2. Blend until smooth.
3. Pour into tall glasses and garnish with roasted crushed peanuts.

Super Green Coconut Detox Smoothie

Serves: 1

Ingredients:

- 1 cup spinach, torn
- ¼ cup fresh orange juice
- ¼ cup pineapple pieces
- 1 kiwifruit, peeled, chopped
- ½ cup ice
- ½ cup coconut milk
- 2 teaspoons chia seeds
- 1 medium banana, sliced
- 2 teaspoons honey
- ½ tablespoon shaved coconut (optional), to garnish

Directions:

1. Add all the ingredients into a blender. Blend until smooth.
2. Pour into tall glasses. Garnish with coconut if using.

Antioxidant Smoothie

Serves: 2

Ingredients:

- 2 cups mixed berries of your choice
- 1 tablespoon chia seeds + extra for garnishing
- 1 cup pomegranate juice, unsweetened
- 1 cup water
- 1 cup ice cubes

Directions:

1. Add berries, chia seeds, pomegranate juice water and ice cubes into a blender and blend until smooth.
2. Pour into tall glasses and serve sprinkled with chia seeds.

Raspberry Oatmeal Smoothie

Serves: 3-4

Ingredients:

- 2 bananas, peeled, sliced
- 1 cup frozen raspberries
- 1 cup old fashioned rolled oats
- ½ cup plain lowfat yogurt
- 2 tablespoons chia seeds
- 2 cups coconut water or water
- 2 tablespoons maple syrup or honey
- Crushed ice

Directions:

1. Add all the ingredients into a blender. Blend until smooth. Add more coconut water if you desire a smoothie of thinner consistency.
2. Pour into tall glasses and serve with crushed ice.

Low Sugar Green Smoothie Bowl

Serves: 1

Ingredients:

- ½ cup coconut milk or coconut milk or unsweetened almond milk
- ½ cup spinach
- 1 ½ cups assorted kale like curly and lacinato, discard hard ribs and stem, torn.
- ½ ripe avocado, peeled, pitted, chopped
- ½ small banana, frozen
- 1 Brazil nut
- ½ teaspoon ground cinnamon
- ¼ teaspoon ground ginger
- ½ date, pitted
- 1 teaspoon moringa powder
- A pinch salt
- ½ scoop protein powder or collagen powder
- 2 teaspoons almond butter
- ½ teaspoon turmeric powder
- Ice cubes as required
- Kiwi slices to serve
- 1 teaspoon chia seeds to serve
- 1 teaspoon coconut flakes, unsweetened to serve

Directions:

1. Add all the ingredients except kiwi slices, chia seeds and coconut flakes into a blender.

2. Blend until smooth.
3. Pour into a bowl. Sprinkle chia seeds and coconut flakes on top. Garnish with kiwi slices and serve.

Quinoa Chia Seed Protein Bars

Serves: 6

Ingredients:

- ¼ cup dry quinoa
- 1 tablespoon ground flax seeds
- A pinch Himalayan salt
- ½ teaspoon ground cardamom
- 2 tablespoons honey
- ¼ cup almond butter
- ¼ cup chia seeds
- ½ cup rolled oats
- ¼ cup almonds, chopped
- 2 tablespoons brown rice syrup

Directions:

1. Add almond butter, honey and brown rice syrup into a microwave safe bowl. Microwave on High for 40-50 seconds or until it melts. Mix well.
2. Add rest of the ingredients into a bowl and stir.
3. Pour the almond butter mixture into it. Mix well. You may have to use your hands to mix.
4. Line a baking dish with parchment paper. Transfer the mixture into the baking dish. Spread it evenly with a spatula. Place the dish in the middle rack of a preheated oven.
5. Bake at 350 F for around 15 minutes.

6. Cool for 10-15 minutes. Remove the baked bar along with the parchment paper and cool on a wire rack.
7. Cut into 6 equal squares and serve.

Power Salad with Lemon Chia Seed Dressing

Serves: 2

Ingredients:

For salad:

- 2 cups packed spinach, torn
- ½ cup cooked quinoa
- ¼ cup almonds, chopped
- ½ cup red cabbage, chopped
- 1 medium sweet potato, peeled, cubed, roasted
- 7.5 ounces canned chickpeas, rinsed, drained
- 1 medium Gala or Fuji apple, cored, diced
- 1 medium avocado, peeled, pitted, sliced

For lemon chia seed dressing:

- 2 tablespoons olive oil
- 1 tablespoon golden or white balsamic vinegar
- 1 teaspoon chia seeds
- Salt to taste
- Freshly ground pepper to taste
- 1 tablespoon fresh lemon juice
- 1 teaspoon honey or agave nectar

Directions:

1. Add all the ingredients of the salad into a bowl and toss well.
2. To make dressing: Add all the ingredients of the dressing into a small jar. Fasten the lid and shake the jar vigorously until the mixture is well combined.
3. Pour over the salad. Toss well and serve.

Chia Seed and Cucumber Salad

Serves: 2

Ingredients:

- 2 Persian cucumbers, trimmed, halved lengthwise, deseeded, sliced
- ½ tablespoon apple cider vinegar
- A pinch granulated sugar
- 2 teaspoons red onion, finely minced (optional)
- 2 tablespoons Greek yogurt
- 1 tablespoon chia seeds
- Salt to taste

Directions:

1. Add cucumber into a bowl. Add rest of the ingredients into the bowl and mix well.
2. Refrigerate for 4-6 hours.
3. Taste and adjust the seasoning if required.

Quinoa Salad with Chipotle Chia Dressing

Serves: 2-3

Ingredients:

- 2 cups water
- ¼ teaspoon salt
- 1 cup quinoa, rinsed
- 1 red bell pepper, chopped
- 1 yellow bell pepper, chopped
- 1 small cucumber, chopped

For chipotle chia dressing:

- ¼ cup fresh or store bought orange juice
- 1 tablespoon olive oil
- 1 teaspoon agave nectar
- 1 clove garlic, minced
- Salt to taste
- 1 ½ tablespoons fresh lime juice
- ½ tablespoon chipotle chiles in adobo sauce, chopped
- ½ tablespoon chia seeds
- ¼ teaspoon ground cumin

Directions:

1. To make dressing: Add all the ingredients of the dressing into a small jar. Fasten the lid and shake the jar vigorously until the mixture is

well combined. Place the jar in the refrigerator and chill until the chia swells.

2. When the chia seeds swells, place a saucepan over medium heat. Add water and bring to the boil.
3. Add quinoa and bring to the boil.
4. Lower heat and cover with a lid. Simmer until quinoa is cooked and all the liquid in the saucepan dries. When done, fluff with a fork. Transfer into a bowl. Let it cool for awhile.
5. Transfer into a large bowl. Add bell peppers and cucumber and mix. Pour dressing on top. Mix well and serve.

Cornmeal & Chia Seed Crusted Tilapia

Serves: 2

Ingredients:

- 2 tilapia fillets, boneless, pat dried
- 2 teaspoons low fat mayonnaise
- ½ teaspoon chia seeds
- Olive oil cooking spray
- Kosher salt to taste
- Pepper to taste
- 6 tablespoons cornmeal
- ¼ teaspoon garlic powder

Directions:

1. Mix together cornmeal, chia seeds, salt, pepper and garlic powder on a plate. Set aside.
2. Place a cooking rack on a baking sheet. Spray the rack with cooking spray.
3. Season the fish with salt and pepper. Spread a teaspoon of mayonnaise on each fish.
4. Carefully dredge the mayonnaise side of the fish in the cornmeal mixture. Press into the mixture well.
5. Place the fish on the rack with the coated side facing up.
6. Bake in a preheated oven at 400 F for 15-20 minutes until the fish is cooked through and the top is crunchy.

Linguine Al Limone with Grilled Chia Chicken

Serves: 6

Ingredients:

- 1/3 cup white chia seeds
- 1 ½ pounds ground chicken
- ½ cup red onion, coarsely grated or minced
- 4 ½ tablespoons extra-virgin olive oil
- 2 teaspoons fresh oregano, minced or 1 teaspoon dried oregano
- 2 teaspoons salt or to taste
- ¾ teaspoon red pepper flakes
- ½ cup half and half
- 3 tablespoons fresh basil, thinly sliced (optional)
- ¾ cup purified water
- 1 cup + 2 tablespoons rolled oats (old fashioned oats)
- ¾ cup Parmigiano – Reggiano cheese
- 1/3 cup flat leaf parsley, finely chopped
- 3 cloves garlic, peeled, minced
- 1 ½ teaspoons freshly ground pepper or to taste
- 18 ounces whole grain linguine
- Juice of 1 ½ lemons
- Zest of 1 ½ lemons, grated

Directions:

1. Add water and chia seeds into a bowl. Stir and set aside for 20 minutes.
2. Add chicken, chia mixture, oats, 1/3-cup cheese, parsley, 3 tablespoons oil, oregano, 1 ½ teaspoons salt, red pepper flakes and ¾ cup black pepper into a large bowl. Mix well.
3. Divide the mixture into 30 equal portions and shape into balls.
4. Grill the balls in a preheated grill for about 15 minutes until brown on the outside and cooked inside. Turn the balls every 3-4 minutes.
5. You can also place the balls on a baking sheet and bake at 475 F for about 20 minutes.
6. Prepare the linguine following the instructions on the package. Retain about 1-½ cups of the cooked water.
7. Add about a cup of the retained water into a saucepan. Add half and half and stir. Place the saucepan over high heat. Bring to the boil.
8. Add remaining cheese, salt, pepper and lemon juice and mix well. Add the pasta and toss until well combined.
9. Divide the pasta among 4 bowls. Place meatballs on top. Garnish with basil and lemon zest. Serve right away.

Lentils with Chia Seeds

Serves: 6

Ingredients:

- 3 tablespoons olive oil
- 1 ½ teaspoons cumin seeds
- 1 ½ teaspoons garlic, minced
- 1 ½ teaspoons turmeric powder
- 3 cups red lentils, rinsed
- 1 teaspoon salt or to taste
- Cooked brown rice to serve
- 2 medium onions, chopped
- ¼ teaspoon ground cardamom
- 3 tablespoons fresh ginger, minced
- 1 fresh jalapeño, sliced
- 1 ½ cans tomatoes
- 5-6 cups vegetable stock
- 2 tablespoons chia seeds
- ½ cup fresh cilantro, chopped

Directions:

1. Place a large saucepan over medium heat. Add oil. When the oil is heated, add onions and sauté until light brown.
2. Add cumin seeds and sauté for a minute.
3. Add garlic and cardamom and sauté until fragrant.

4. Add water, turmeric, ginger, jalapeño, stock, tomatoes and lentils and bring to the boil.
5. Lower heat and cover with a lid. Simmer until the lentils are tender.
6. Add chia seeds, salt, and cilantro. Stir and serve over brown rice.

Chia Seed Wafer Cookie

Serves: 2

Ingredients:

- 1 ½ cups chia seeds, lightly toasted
- 2 egg whites
- 1 cup agave nectar
- 1 cup flour
- ½ teaspoon baking powder
- ½ cup whipped butter, softened
- 1 cup coconut sugar
- 1 teaspoon vanilla extract
- ½ teaspoon salt

Directions:

1. Add all the ingredients into a bowl and mix well.
2. Line a baking sheet with parchment paper.
3. Drop tablespoonful of batter on the baking sheet. Leave a gap of about 1-½ inches between 2 cookies.
4. Bake in a preheated oven at 375 F for 6-8 minutes.
5. Remove from the oven and cool for 2 minutes. Remove the cookies from the parchment paper and place on a cooling rack.
6. Transfer into an airtight container.

Tropical Coconut Mango Chia Pudding

Serves: 3

Ingredients:

For chia pudding:

- 1 ¼ cups plain coconut milk, chilled
- 1 teaspoon vanilla extract
- ½ tablespoon grated coconut
- A pinch powdered cardamom
- 6 tablespoons chia seeds
- 2 teaspoons honey or maple syrup
- ¼ teaspoon ground cinnamon

For coconut mango puree:

- 1 medium mango, peeled, pitted, chopped
- 4 teaspoons grated coconut
- 3-4 teaspoons honey

For topping:

- 1 tablespoon shaved coconut, toasted

Directions:

1. To make chia pudding: Add coconut milk, vanilla, coconut, chia seeds, honey and spices into a bowl. Mix well.
2. Cover and refrigerate for 4-8 hours.
3. To make coconut mango puree: Add mango, grated coconut and honey into a blender and blend until smooth.

4. Pour into a bowl and chill for a couple of hours.
5. To assemble: Take 3 glasses. Spoon in about a tablespoon of mango puree alternating with chia seed pudding in each glass. Make layers in this manner until all the puree and chia seeds are used.
6. Sprinkle coconut shaving on top.
7. Chill until use.

Can you help me?

If you enjoyed this book, then we really appreciate it if you would post a short review on Amazon. We read all the reviews and your feedbacks will help us improve our future books.

If you want to leave a private feedback, please email your feedback to: feedback@dingopublishing.com

Thanks for your support!

Now, let's continue on next page.

Conclusion

We come to the end of this book. I hope the information wasn't too heavy. This book will have given you an overview about the most common reasons behind cancer and the simple ways to help prevent it crawling into your body. If you follow the anti-cancer diet and try using the simple recipes in your daily life, it will be helpful in preventing cancer in your life.

The book has covered the primary objective which is to give the readers an idea about how "food can act as a medicine and an energizer" to lead a healthy lifestyle. You can use this recipe book to try out anti-cancer food items on your diet chart and make your meals interesting. Most of these items are easily available on the market at a reasonable price and, as mentioned in the beginning, always go for organic and unprocessed food items.

Remember your body is not a dustbin. Treat your body as a temple and help it give positive vibrations to your soul by eating the right quality of food. Don't humiliate your body with unhealthy food consumption.

I sincerely hope that this book was useful and has helped answer most of the queries you had in your mind. My best wishes to you to lead a healthy cancer-free life. Eat the right food and stay healthy. Satisfy your taste buds by eating the food, which not only feeds your body but also feeds your soul. I once again thank you for purchasing this book!

Before you go, I have a surprise for you on next page!

BONUS

As a way of saying thanks for your purchase, I'm offering a special gift that's exclusive to my readers.

Claim your bonus from the link below:

http://bit.ly/VBonus1

Another surprise! There are free sample chapters of our **best-selling** book at the end:

Anti-inflammatory Diet For Beginners
by Jonathan Smith

MORE BOOKS FROM US

Chia Seeds Cookbook

Kale Cookbook

Intermittent Fasting by Jonathan Smith

HIIT – High Intensity Interval training
by Joshua King

Procrastination by J. Martin

Accelerated learning by Jason Clark

BONUS

Sample chapters of 'Anti-Inflammatory Diet For Beginner' by Jonathan Smith.

Introduction

These days, everywhere you go and every website you visit, you are going to find discussions or adverts about this or that diet program. Diets that can help you lose weight, diets that can cure cancer, and even diets that promise to increase your bank account. Some of these diets work; others are a waste of your time, energy, and financial resources. The anti-inflammatory diet is nothing like these fad diets. This revolutionary diet draws upon a simple scientific and biographical logic guaranteed to work for you regardless of your circumstances.

The anti-inflammatory diet has many innate benefits including lowering your risk of heart diseases, protecting the bones, helping you maintain a healthy weight, and increasing your body's ability to absorb nutrients from the foods you eat and the drugs you take.

This book is a comprehensive guide that shall impart upon you everything you need to know about the anti-inflammatory diet. Let's begin.

Chapter 1: Introduction to the Anti-Inflammatory Diet

To make this book easy to read and follow, we will start by understanding inflammation and the anti-inflammatory diet.

In its simplest terms, an anti-inflammatory diet simply refers to a collection of foods that have the ability to fight off chronic inflammation in your body.

So what exactly is chronic inflammation?

Well, before we discuss that, let's start by understanding what inflammation is first.

So what is inflammation?

Inflammation is simply a term used to refer to your body's response to infection, injuries, imbalance, or irritation with the response being swelling, soreness, heat, or loss of body function. It is the body's first line of defence against bacteria, viruses and various other ailments. The goal is to 'quarantine' the area and bring about healing/relief. This is the good inflammation, as it is helpful to your body. It is often referred to as acute inflammation. However, there are times when the inflammatory process might not work as expected resulting to a cascade of activities that could ultimately result to cell and tissue damage especially if it takes place over a prolonged period. This is what's referred to as chronic inflammation. This type of inflammation has nothing to do with injuries; it is not as a result of an injury or anything related to bacteria, virus or any other microbe. And unlike acute inflammation that comes with soreness, pain, heat and swelling, chronic inflammation comes with another set of symptoms some of which include diarrhoea, skin outbreaks, congestion, dry eyes, headaches, loss of joint function and many others. This inflammation is what you need to fight using an anti-inflammatory diet because if it is not addressed early, it might result to a number of various chronic health complications that we will discuss in a while.

So how exactly does this chronic inflammation develop that would actually require a diet to undo? Here is how:

It all starts in the gut. The gut essentially has a large semi-porous lining, which tends to fluctuate depending on various chemicals that it comes into contact with. For instance, if exposed to cortisol, a hormone that is high when you are stressed, the lining becomes more permeable. The lining also becomes a lot more permeable depending on the changing levels of thyroid hormones. This increased permeability increases the likelihood of viruses, bacteria, yeast, toxins and various digested foods passing through the intestines to get into the bloodstream, a phenomenon referred to as leaky gut syndrome (LGS). The thing is, if this (the intestinal lining becomes damaged repetitively), the microvilli in the gut start getting crippled such that they cannot do their job well i.e. processing and using nutrients with some enzymes that are effective for proper digestion. This essentially makes your digestive system weaker a phenomenon that results to poor absorption of nutrients. If foreign substances find their way into the bloodstream through the wrong channels, this results to an immune response that could result to inflammation and allergic reactions. This form of inflammation can bring about different harmful complications. What's worse is that as inflammation increases, the body keeps on producing more white blood cells to fight off the foreign bodies that have found their way into the bloodstream. This can go on for a long time resulting to malfunctioning of different organs, nerves, joints, muscles, and connective tissues.

Chronic inflammation is harmful to your body and your brain. Let me explain more of this:

Your body is responsible for supplying glucose to your brain so that your brain can perform optimally. When you eat too much inflammation-causing foods, your body slows down its process of transporting glucose to the brain since it concentrates on fighting off the inflammation. Your brain then keeps asking the body for glucose since it is not getting its fill. This effect causes you to crave sugary and pro-inflammatory foods. Inflammation can also result to abnormal levels of water retention along with other problems that contribute to stubborn weight gain. This just worsens the condition and causes your inflammation to worsen. Unfortunately, majorities of dieters focused on weight loss only focus on reducing calories and fatty foods but pay very little attention to how eating pro-inflammatory foods may be contributing to an inability to lose weight quickly.

If inflammation persists, it can bring about a wide array of health complications some of which include:

- Obesity and chronic weight gain
- Lupus
- Arthritis
- Cancer
- Diabetes
- Celiac disease

- Crohn's disease
- Heart disease

So how exactly does inflammation lead to disease? That's what we will discuss next.

How Inflammation Could Lead to Diseases

It is possible to have a disease-free body, but only if you can manage to keep your body balanced. Diseases develop only when something upsets the equilibrium (balance) of the body. An abnormal composition of blood and nymph is a typical example of such imbalance. These two are responsible for supplying the tissues with nutrients and carrying away eliminated toxins, metabolic by-products and wastes from the liver and kidneys. When you consume unhealthy meals, it may affect the balance of blood and nymph in the body and lead to inadequate supply of nutrients and thus, the body would be unable to give adequate support to kidney and liver function. The consequence of this is that it exposes the body to the risks of several diseases and inflammatory conditions, which I mentioned earlier.

Food Allergies, Food Intolerance, and the Anti-Inflammatory Diet

Food allergies happen when your immune system reacts to the proteins in certain foods. Your immune system releases histamines that may cause production of throat mucous, runny nose, watery eyes, and in severe cases, diarrhea, hives, and anaphylaxis.

Your immune system's reaction to food allergies is to trigger inflammatory responses because when a food causes allergic reaction, it stimulates the production of antibodies that bind to the foods and may cross-react with the normal tissues in your body.

One of the highpoints of the anti-inflammatory diet is that it calls for the elimination of foods that promote allergies and intolerance.

How the Anti-Inflammatory Diet Works

To cure and stop incessant inflammation, you must eliminate the irritation and infection, and correct hormonal imbalance by eating specific foods while avoiding others. This would help stop the destruction of cells and hyperactive response of your immune system. When on an anti-inflammatory diet, most of the foods you shall be eating have powerful antioxidants that can help prevent and eliminate symptoms of inflammation.

For instance, anti-inflammatory foods such as avocados contain Glutathione, a powerful antioxidant. Radishes contain Indol-3-Carbinol (13C), which increases the flow of blood to injured areas. Pomegranates have polyphenols that stop the enzyme reactions the body uses to trigger inflammation. Shiitake Mushrooms are high in polyphenols that protect the liver cells from damage. Ginger has hormones that help ease inflammation pain.

We will discuss more on the foods you should eat and those you should avoid later.

In the next chapter, we shall look at the basic rules of the anti-inflammatory diet as well as how to get the best out of the diet program.

Chapter 2: Basic Rules of the Anti-Inflammatory Diet

As is the case with any diet, the anti-inflammatory diet has basic rules but as you are about to find out, these rules are very easy to follow and straightforward: no extreme rules that would leave you cravings-crazy and running back to a poor eating style after a few days.

When following this diet, there are about 11 rules you should follow:

1st: You Must Eat at Least 25 Grams of Fiber Daily

These should be whole grain fibrous foods such as oatmeal and barley, vegetables such as eggplant, onions, and okra, and fruits like blueberries and bananas. These fiber-rich foods have naturally occurring phytonutrients that help fight inflammation.

2nd: Eat at Least Nine Servings of Fruits and Vegetables Daily

A serving of fruit refers to half a cup of fruits while a serving of vegetable refers to a cup of leafy green vegetables. You could also add some herbs and spices such as ginger, cinnamon, and turmeric, foods that have strong anti-inflammatory and antioxidant properties.

3rd: Eat at Least Four Servings of Crucifers and Alliums Every Week

Crucifers refer to vegetables such as Brussels sprouts, Broccoli, mustard greens, Cabbage, and Cauliflower. Alliums refer to onions, garlic, scallions, and leek. These foods have strong anti-inflammatory properties and may even lower risks of cancer. You should eat at least four servings of these every day, and at least one clove of garlic daily.

4th: Consume Only 10% of Saturated Fat Daily

The average daily recommended calories for adults is about 2,000 calories every day. This means you have to limit your daily saturated fat caloric intake to no more than 200 calories. If you consume less than 2,000 calories daily, you have to reduce accordingly.

Saturated fats include foods like hydrogenated and partially hydrogenated oils, pork, desserts and baked goods, sausages, fried chicken and full fat diary. Saturated fats often contain toxic compounds that promote inflammation, which is why you need to eliminate these foods from your diet.

5th: Eat a Lot of Omega-3 Fatty Acid Rich Foods

Omega-3 fatty acids rich foods such as walnuts, kidney, navy and soybeans, flaxseed, sardines, salmon, herring, oysters, mackerel and anchovies are an essential part of this diet thanks to their strong anti-inflammatory properties.

6th: Eat Fish Thrice Weekly

It is important that you eat cold-water fish and low-fat fish at least three times a week because fishes are rich sources of healthy fats and can be great substitutes for saturated and unhealthy fats.

7th: Use Healthier Oils

The fact that you have to reduce your intake of some types of fat does not mean you should stop consuming all fats. You only need to reduce or even eliminate the consumption of unhealthy ones and limit your intake of healthy ones like expeller pressed canola, sunflower and safflower oil, and virgin olive oil. These oils have anti-oxidant properties that help detoxify the body.

8th: Eat Healthy Snacks at Least Twice Daily

Unlike in most diets, in this diet, you get to eat snacks as long as it is healthy. You can snack on healthy foods such Greek Yoghurt, almonds, celery sticks, pistachios, and carrots.

9th: Reduce Consumption of Processed Foods and Refined Sugars

Reducing your intake of artificial sweeteners and refined sugars can help alleviate insulin resistance and lower risks of blood pressure. It may also help reduce uric acid levels in your body. Having too much uric acid in your body may lead to gout, kidney stones, and even cancer. A high level of uric acid in the body is usually because of poor kidney function. Overloading your kidneys with pro-inflammatory foods may reduce kidney function and subsequently lead to excessive uric acid levels in the body.

Reducing your consumption of refined sugars and foods high in sodium can help reduce inflammation caused by excess uric acid within the body.

10th: Reduce Consumption of Trans Fat

Studies by the FDA reveal that foods high in trans-fat have higher levels of C-reactive protein, a biomarker for inflammation in the body. Foods like cookies and crackers, margarines, and any products with partially or fully hydrogenated oils are some of the foods with high trans-fat content.

11th: Use Fruits and Spices to Sweeten Your Meals

Instead of using sugar and harmful ingredients to sweeten your meals, use fruits that can act as natural sweeteners such as berries, apples, apricot, cinnamon, turmeric, ginger, sage, cloves, thyme, and rosemary.

Now that we have laid down the rules, the next thing we will do is to put what we've learnt into perspective i.e. what foods you should eat and what you should avoid. The next chapter has a comprehensive list of foods to consume and foods to avoid while on this diet. Consider printing out the chapter so you can use it as a reference each time you need to cook or make shopping decisions. If you do, it will not be long before you get used to the diet and can quickly decipher foods which foods you should and should not buy.

Chapter 3: Eat These, Not These

The whole gist of what we have been discussing all along is how inflammation is an obvious sign that something has upset your body's balance and that the headache, body pain, weight gain, and joint pain, excessive food cravings, and digestion problems that you always experience are not there by accident.

Something we are yet to discuss is the issues of acidity versus alkalinity. It is also very important that you maintain a healthy pH level in the body. Some pro-inflammatory are mostly acidic and when you consume these foods, it offsets the balance of acid and alkaline in your body, which could also trigger inflammation.

When you eat anti-inflammatory foods that are mostly alkaline, your body will feel more energetic, healthy, and free from diseases. Your digestive system would be free from clogs and function optimally. This further promotes an anti-inflammatory body.

The table below shows the pro-inflammatory foods and those that are anti-inflammatory. From this table, you can clearly see the foods you should be eating and those ones you should avoid on this diet.

With this table in your hands, you can plan your meals outside of the diet plan and recipes you will find in the next chapter.

The table has three columns. The first row has a list of foods you can eat with reckless abandon. These foods have immense health benefits besides the fact that they are anti-inflammatory.

The second row has a list of foods you should eat sparingly. You could limit your consumption of these to a few times a week or special occasions.

In the last row, you shall find a list of foods you should not eat as long as you are on this diet. These meals trigger an inflammatory response and have other consequences on your health.

Eat These	**Eat These on Special Occasions Only**	**Don't Even Dare Touch These**
Leafy greens e.g. collard greens, kale, romaine, kale, Swiss chard, green leaf lettuce, red leaf lettuce and spinach	Salad dressings	Foods that contain sugar, those that are sweet and those that are converted into sugar (glucose) during digestion e.g. breads, alcohol, white potatoes and rice.
Shellfish e.g. oysters, shrimp and scallops	Dark chocolate	Foods high in trans fats like margarine, packaged foods like cakes mixes and biscuit mixes with high trans fat per serving. You will find trans-fats in deep fried foods e.g. deep fried

		fish, chicken, French fries etc.
Dark green and cruciferous vegetables e.g. celery, broccoli, zucchini, cauliflower, turnip, Brussels sprouts, cabbage, bok choy, arugula, watercress, rutabaga, cucumber etc.	Vinegars except apple cider vinegar	Red meat
Lemon and lime	Dried fruits with sulfite or sugar added.	Sodas and energy drinks
Herbs and spices e.g. Basil, cayenne, ginger, turmeric, garlic, and oregano.	Wheat	Foods high in saturated fats like: dairy products (whole) and full fat dairy products, source cream, butter, cheese, and whole milk.

		Others include red meat (e.g. pork, lamp, canned meats, bacon, fried meats, beef, lard, organ meats etc.
Beans and legumes (soak first and then properly-prepare before eating)	Maple, agave, coconut, or other natural sugars	All fast foods
Stevia glycerite or alcohol-free stevia	Roasted seeds and nuts	Beer and other alcoholic drinks
Protein powders (non-GMO and whole-food based)	Non-soaked grains and non-sprouted grains excluding millet and wild rice	Coffee (except for low-acid coffee)
Raw seeds and nuts like sesame seeds, hazelnuts, and hempseeds	Roasted nut butters	Highly processed foods and snacks including chips and low-quality

		cereals
Raw nuts and butters	Soy-based proteins including tofu, veggie burgers, and tempeh) You could eat whole forms of soy like edamame, and fermented miso.	Artificial and processed sugars including stevia with added GMO or maltodextrin, aspartame, cane juice and sugar, brown sugar, white sugar, sucralose, sucrose, and dextrose)
Coconut oil and olive oil		Processed soy
Fruits like dates, pineapples, apples, papaya, Dried figs, oranges, watermelon, kiwi fruit, tomatoes, berries like blueberries, strawberries and cranberries, raspberries,		Refined grains

cherries, blackberries, pomegranates, etc.		
White meat sources like pork, poultry (chicken, turkey, quails etc.) fish etc.		Nicotine/drugs
Mushrooms e.g. Asian and Shiitake mushrooms		
Traditional food and fermented vegetables like Kimchi, Sauerkraut and kefir, miso, natto, tempeh, pickles and olives		
Wild millet and wild rice		
Apple cider vinegar		
Herbal tea and		

matcha tea etc.		
Seaweed including spirulina, dulse and kelp.		
Fresh and clean water		
Omega 3 fatty acid rich foods such as: boiled or baked tuna, sardines, salmon, and mackerel: hemp seeds, chia seeds, avocados, olives and walnuts		
Other anti-inflammatory foods like quinoa, oatmeal, green tea, pistachios, eggs, almonds, beets, pumpkin, leeks and lentils		

In addition to the above foods to eat and those to avoid, you can also use supplements to help fight inflammation. For instance, you can use vitamin D, vitamin B, C and E.

Please note that the idea behind this diet is not to achieve a 100% anti-inflammatory diet. That is almost impossible to achieve because you are human and shall certainly experience some undying cravings. The idea is to eat a 90% anti-inflammatory diet. The rest of the 10% leaves wiggle room for some of the foods you cannot do without food items as coffee, almond milk, and so on.

Chapter 4:
Health Benefits of the Anti-Inflammatory Diet

Improved Brain Performance

Chronic inflammation may affect the brain and cause mental exhaustion. In turn, mental exhaustion may trigger feelings of depression, anxiety, and indecisiveness.

When you eat too much processed foods, bad fats, carbs and sugar, it may cause some blood sugar abnormalities that could cause insulin resistance. Insulin resistance may cause altered gastrointestinal function that may negatively affect normal brain function.

When you stop eating pro-inflammatory foods and start eating anti-inflammatory foods, it gives your brain a health boost because you would be eating anti-oxidant-rich foods that increase your brain function instead of impairing it.

Improved Skin Texture and Appearance

The skin is the largest organ in the body and as such, whatever you eat negatively or positively affects the skin. A poor diet may trigger skin inflammatory conditions. For instance, eating processed foods, sugar, and bad fats can cause leaky gut, something that forms from an imbalanced gut flora. Leaky gut could increase inflammation in the body and then cause skin problems like acne, itchiness, psoriasis, dull skin, and rosacea and skin rashes.

When you eliminate pro-inflammatory foods and introduce the foods you will be eating while on the anti-inflammatory diet, your skin appearance shall improve, so shall be your skin's texture with the resultant effect being a glowing and fresh looking skin.

Improved Weight Loss and Control of Cravings

Excessive food cravings are the reason why most people find it difficult to lose weight. The thing is; consumption of sugar and starch increases your cravings. Sugar cravings are not normal; it simply shows something is out of balance within your body system. Consuming excess sugars sets off a vicious cycle of food and sugar cravings that affects the chemicals in your brain. The more you continue consuming sugary foods, the worse the situation gets and the more your body becomes susceptible to inflammation.

The foods the anti-inflammatory diet advocates for help reduce cravings. Spices such as cinnamon, cloves, and cardamom have properties that help you control cravings. When you effectively reduce and control your cravings, you will lose weight because reduced cravings lead to a reduction in the calories you consume and eventually, reduced calorie consumption leads to weight loss.

An anti-inflammatory diet shall also see you eliminate many of the foods that make it difficult for you to lose weight. It also eliminates insulin and leptin resistance, which affects metabolism and promotes weight gain.

Reduction of Bloating

Foods like gluten and dairy products promote bloating. This is because of something called Dysbiosis. Dysbiosis refers to a situation where bad microorganisms overshadow good microorganisms. There should be a balance in the community of microorganisms in your gut. However, consumption of inflammatory foods promotes the growth of bad bacteria with the resultant effect being excessive bloating.

Dysbiosis can also occur when bacteria gets into the small intestines. Some anti-inflammatory foods have probiotics that increase the growth and spread of good bacteria that rectify and reverse the imbalance in your gut so you no longer feel bloated.

Prevents Autoimmunity

According to recent statistics, about 50 million Americans suffer from autoimmune disorders. Autoimmunity refers to a health condition where your immune system erroneously identifies your cells and tissues as harmful, and begins working against them. Inflammatory foods create antibodies that may trigger autoimmunity; hence, phasing out inflammatory foods and incorporating anti-inflammatory ones could help you stop consuming foods that may trigger autoimmune responses since most anti-inflammatory foods have detoxifying properties that help eliminate the antibodies before your immune system can start reacting.

Cures Adrenal Fatigue

Some of the most important hormones your body needs to be healthy include the Aldosterone and Cortisol. Cortisol controls and aids metabolism while aldosterone contributes to the regulation of blood pressure. The adrenal glands are responsible for producing these two hormones. Any malfunction of the adrenal glands affects the entire body system.

If your body becomes severely inflamed, something bound to happen when you consume excess amounts of refined carbs, adrenal fatigue may occur. Some symptoms of adrenal fatigue include depression, weight gain, anxiety, fatigue, inability to focus, excessive food cravings, burnouts, and difficulty getting out of bed.

Removing inflammatory foods from your diet can help boost adrenal system function and alleviate the symptoms of adrenal fatigue.

Alleviation of Allergies

Inflammatory foods may compromise your gut and make your body more susceptible to food allergies. The anti-inflammatory diet asks that you consume less of foods that may increase food allergies (such as food additives, fermented foods, processed meats, soy sauce, yeasty food, white wine, and beer).

One of the greatest things about the anti-inflammatory diet is that to derive these benefits, you need not do a complete overhaul of your regular diet. You simply need to incorporate beneficial foods and eliminate the harmful ones: no starvation, and no calorie counting. I believe you have realized just how easy it is to follow an anti-inflammatory diet. You can combine what you have learnt with several lifestyle changes for greater effectiveness. Some of the lifestyle changes you can embrace include:

- Reducing stress: Remember cortisol, the stress hormone, is highly inflammatory if it lingers for too long. Also, stress affects the adrenal glands negatively resulting to inflammatory responses if the problem sticks around for too long.

- Getting enough sleep: This will greatly help you to restore the much needed balance, which will provide a friendly environment for fighting inflammation effortlessly.

- Being physically active: This will help you to fight stress, enhance metabolism, protect your muscles, protect the heart and much more. Physical activity also helps to strengthen your immune system.

- Getting enough water: Water is very important in the process of fighting inflammation as it helps in the removal of toxins, improves digestion and enhances brain function.

Also, make sure to reduce your exposure to various toxins as these can easily trigger inflammatory responses. You can do that by giving up some bad habits that expose you to toxins like smoking, taking alcohol, drug use etc.

*********END OF SAMPLE CHAPTERS*********

Anti-inflammatory Diet for Beginners by Jonathan Smith

Thanks again for purchasing this book.
I hope you enjoy it!

Made in the USA
Columbia, SC
29 May 2019